FAMILY GARDENS

HOW TO CREATE MAGICAL OUTDOOR SPACES FOR ALL AGES

FAMILY GARDENS

HOW TO CREATE MAGICAL OUTDOOR SPACES FOR ALL AGES

BUNNY GUINNESS

D&C
David and Charles

Editor: Emily Pitcher
Project Editor: Katie Hardwicke
Desk Editor: Demelza Hookway
Designer: Eleanor Stafford
Production Controller: Beverley Richardson
Illustrations: Kevin Hart

Visit our website at www.davidandcharles.co.uk

David & Charles books are available from all good
bookshops; alternatively you can contact our Orderline on
0870 9908222 or write to us at FREEPOST EX2 110, D&C
Direct, Newton Abbot, TQ12 4ZZ (no stamp required
UK only); US customers call 800-289-0963 and Canadian
customers call 800-840-5220.

All photographs copyright © Juliette Wade, except p. 101
copyright © Bunny Guinness, p. 108 copyright © Garden
Picture Library. and cover image copyright Digital Visions/
Punchstock..

TO MY CHILDREN
UNITY AND FREDDIE

CONTENTS..............

INTRODUCTION

The final nudge that propelled me into action on this book was my son's fourth birthday party. We had organized a clown to entertain the children's friends and as it was a sunny day we decided that the fun and games could take place in our small back garden. As we settled back into our chairs, looking forward to some gentle amusement, chaos erupted around us. The clown, who normally has all onlookers spellbound, was totally ignored – indeed, no one even seemed aware of his presence. All the children were immersed (some literally) in the attractions of the water garden – reeds, frogs, fish, dragonflies, snails, pebbles and sludge. After an hour of trying to attract attention away from this wildlife extravaganza the poor entertainer gave up, muttering, 'There is just no way anyone could compete with that.'

Of course he was right. An enticing garden can offer children a vast amount of scope for thrills, spills and excitement, far more than the confines of orchestrated entertainment, no matter how good. But how often do you see gardens that are planned around the whole family? We seem to veer between extremes: either the whole garden becomes merely an area to contain plastic climbing frames and the like that make any attempt to create an attractive garden impossible, or else any hint of family fun is banished, sacrificed to the cause of a garden that is purely for admiring.

Now that people tend to be more established in their own homes before their first child comes on the scene, there has usually been time to make the best use of all the space, inside and out. It seems a shame to go back to square one with the garden and banish all thoughts of aesthetic values once the family begins to grow. This precious outdoor area may be the only safe space available where children can play without a watchful adult breathing down their necks, and they spend thousands of hours here with their parents, siblings and friends. Yet most families spend fewer hours, less thought and far less money on fulfilling the potential of their garden than they do on indoor toys and computer games, many of which become discarded all too quickly.

I have aimed to describe in this book how to design and create a garden that will have elements to inspire everyone, from hyperactive ball players to green-fingered artists. I have tried to stress how important it is to get the whole family involved, so that everyone has a vested interest in the garden. After all, every member of the family must have one part of it that strikes a chord, even if it's only the position of the hammock!

DESIGN AND PLANNING

No garden can be a real success unless the overall design is right. This is particularly true of the family garden, which must cater for both children and adults with radically different ideas about the purpose of the plot of land outside the door. At the same time, the garden must look good while requiring no more maintenance than you are comfortably able to provide. It is often not feasible to create the whole garden at once, but as long as you have a cohesive plan at the outset, the work may be carried out in stages as time and finances allow.

ENJOYING YOUR GARDEN

Adults generally have a good idea about what they want from their garden – whether it be a beautiful, tranquil oasis where eating and entertaining can take place outside, or a plantsman's paradise. However, most adults also appreciate that what children want from a garden is equally important and essential to harmonious family life. This book will show how your child's desire to climb trees, make dens, ride bicycles and kick balls need not conflict with your own garden dreams.

Making the most of a garden

Even without climbing apparatus, ball games and sand pits, the garden environment has much to offer children. It appeals to all the senses with bright colours, exotic perfumes, interesting sounds, tactile plants and plenty to taste in the vegetable garden. An added bonus is that a garden is continually changing. Exciting events happen every day: sunflowers bloom, birds hatch, dandelion clocks scatter, frogspawn arrives and bumble bees feed from foxgloves.

However, for a family to make the most of these natural pleasures, a garden must be well designed. It is here that children will create a secret fantasy play world, while adults find peace in the potager or potting shed. There should also be areas that encourage the family to come together, such as a terrace, pool or seating area. If the garden is well planned, life can be idyllic with children happily and constructively occupied outside from dawn to dusk.

The value of outdoor play

Toddlers and young children discover new things every day. They are developing their senses and learning physical skills, usually by touching, tasting, testing, grasping and climbing, or simply observing. Adventures of this sort must often be discouraged indoors where space is limited and precious things hard to repair. In the garden, however, safe areas can be created to allow children to develop vital skills and give full rein to their desire for investigation. Sand pits let children weigh, mix, pour and tunnel, while a water feature gives them a continual source of absorbing interest, not only from splashing about but also through watching wildlife.

A playhouse or tree house is the child's domain, where they can 'live' in the manner they most enjoy and escape the confines of the house. Climbing and swinging structures, dens, pets and various games can all be far better accommodated outside, and they can be designed to blend in well with the garden.

An old stone sink provides an ideal work-and-play area, which is also used for sailing toy boats.

Children and gardening

A creative way to harness children's energy is to encourage them to garden. Spend time gardening with them, letting them do the choice bits – giving them seeds that are easy to grow and bedding plants on the point of flowering.

Children will attack projects only in short bursts initially. Recognize their short attention span and make gardening fairly action-packed so as to arouse and develop their enthusiasm. As they become more interested, do not be surprised to discover that a mini vegetable plot or palatial pool for a family of newts has found a place in your back garden.

Involve children in each stage of the garden's development from planning to planting. Leaf through gardening books together, take them to other gardens, parks and wild areas and see which 'habitats' are appreciated most. Plan dens and hideaways that offer more potential for play and adventure than an indoor playroom. Encourage them to draw sketches of tree houses, paddling pools and climbing trees, and make use of these whenever it is practical, so that they feel they have contributed to the garden's development and you feel that you are fulfilling some of their dreams.

This jungle-like mass of bamboo and other plants provides a tranquil hideaway for reading and dreaming.

In this garden, a raised walkway and cable runway link up with a tree house, leaving the lawn free for ball games.

The Changing Garden

Whether you are making changes to an existing garden, or creating a new garden from scratch, the cardinal rules, to my mind, are: a) to set out an overall plan before you start to make any alterations; b) to tackle the improvements over a comparatively long period of time (such as ten years or more); and c) to retain an element of flexibility so that the garden grows with you.

With an overall master plan you can ensure that all the elements of your garden will eventually complement one another. For example, if the plan has an area designated as a conservatory but you do not yet have the funds to build one, in the meantime make sure that the garden surrounding that area will fit in beautifully when your conservatory is in place.

To arrive at the overall master plan, each member of the family should decide what they would ideally like to have in their garden. Once this list is built up it will need to be edited until it matches what is practical and possible in terms of space and budget. Adults and children are likely to have different preferences (see chart, right).

Few people are lucky enough to have both the space and money for everything they would like in the garden, but think again before excluding features that you think are unachievable. If you crave a woodland garden, much can be achieved in a small space. If you have, for example, a 3m (9ft) wide strip of land along a boundary, careful selection and close planting of young, inexpensive 600–900mm (2–3ft) tall trees will produce a woodland edge habitat easily within ten years. It will be an attractive natural play space, a wonderful backdrop to the garden – perhaps hiding a neighbouring eyesore – and a delightful wildlife habitat.

Adaptable play features

Some garden play features can easily be adapted to another use once the children have outgrown them. With a modern butyl liner, sand pits can quickly be converted into ornamental or wildlife pools. A climbing structure can be designed to function as a pergola at a later date (see pp. 52-53), and climbing plants, provided they are sited sensibly, can be grown around the structure from day one. As parents become grandparents, a summer house can be easily adapted so that it also functions as a playhouse – perhaps by fitting a small door inside the adults' door, like a judas gate, and adding miniature tables and chairs. A tree house might start off near to the ground for young children and be extended with ladders and ever higher storeys as the children grow.

Adults' requirements	Children's requirements
• Sheltered eating and entertaining area	• Playhouse or den
• Barbecue	• Space to pitch a tent
• Tranquil place in which to relax	• Climbing frame
• Water feature	• Tree house
• A screen from neighbours	• Sand pit
• Kitchen garden area with vegetables	• Paddling pool
• Garden room for office or studio	• Wildlife pool
• Shed for storage	• Area of long grass for stalking games
• Greenhouse to allow plant propagation	• Place to ride bikes
• Lawn	• Woodland for games and privacy
• Woodland area	• Stream or bogland ditch for games
• Orchard	• Flowering borders that attract bees and butterflies
• Herb garden	• Pet area
• Japanese garden	• Vegetable or flower plot
• Herbaceous borders	• Area for ball games
• Area for pets/chickens	• Swimming pool
• Private place to sunbathe	• Swing
	• Trees for climbing

This climbing structure of rustic poles is an ideal feature for a family garden, combining interest for the children with an attractive appearance.

This small playhouse is perched on top of a boundary fence; it has been built by two neighbouring families for their children to share, with access from both gardens.

Swinging tyres can be added to trees and structures to give good play value, simply and inexpensively.

THE MASTER PLAN

To make a successful master plan, you must bear a number of elements in mind: the needs of adults and children; the amount of maintenance you can provide; the requirements of wildlife; and, of course, visual appeal. Different areas of the garden will have different functions and therefore different characters, creating interest and contrast, yet they must add up to a unified whole.

Make sure that you have highlighted all the advantages of your garden (fine views, changes in level, natural water, charming old fruit trees, and so on) and have come to grips with its problems (lack of privacy, lack of shelter, ugly views of your own or your neighbour's house). Think about all the pluses and minuses and mark them up on an overall layout of the garden.

The house is often the most dominant feature in a garden. The first thing to do is to make a critical appraisal of your house's good and bad features. As you are going to be continually viewing your house from the garden, you want to direct the eye to its best features and mask out any eyesores with attractive planting.

Design components

It can be quite a challenge to incorporate all the elements you want into a cohesive design. Unless the area is very small, you will probably have to break the garden up into different spaces by means of fences, planting, pergolas, hedges, paving or levels. Try to decide what feel or character you want to create in each space, and how they will flow into each other.

Deciding which features to put where will usually require a bit of juggling. Logic may dictate certain things, such as a herb garden near the back door, enabling some elements to fall into the best place fairly easily. If you can designate a separate area for children, make it a slightly private and wilder place where you can hide some of their activities with tough planting.

Make areas of mixed planting accessible for children and adults by means of a network of narrow informal paths and tough plants.

In this area of paving, the lavish planting is visually dominant. The generous expanse of hard surface looks good all year round.

Paving A paved area is often adjacent to the house, so its design must be complementary to the building. Do not make this paved area too small as it will probably be well used and also highly visible from the house. Try to avoid the use of just one type of material; instead break up the paving with patterns and planting.

Lawn If you have the space, do include an area of lawn that can be used by all the family, perhaps for ball games that can be enjoyed by everyone. However, try not to surround it with your most prize-worthy borders, and use tougher plants on the edges.

Water The water feature is another aspect that everyone will find attractive. It is perhaps most important to site it where it can be easily appreciated from the house so you can watch the wildlife it attracts.

Vegetable patch Providing a separate area for growing vegetables and herbs is a worthwhile use of space. Consider siting this area near the kitchen door and laying out a series of small beds in an appealing pattern, divided by narrow paths. Add a few attractive elements to the area – a seat, some runner bean wigwams, a raised sink in which to wash the produce, some sweet peas, sunflowers and nasturtiums. Then, no doubt, you'll all end up wanting to sit in it.

When you think you have arrived at an overall layout for the garden, mark the design out on the ground with canes and string and live with the anticipated alterations in this form for a while to make sure that they will function in the way you hope; it can be a take to bring in the bulldozers straight away.

KEY

Gravel with plants

Mixed border

Flowering meadow

Mown grass

Hedges

Here, areas of different character are separated by different levels.

N

A TOWN GARDEN PLAN
This garden belongs to a family with six children. They all enjoy the games lawn, and the paved eating area is conveniently sited outside the French windows to the kitchen. At the far end a wildlife area with a pool and garden building provides a peaceful hideaway.

Disguising Utilities

Most family gardens have their fair share of eyesores, including telegraph poles, compost heaps, rabbit hutches, greenhouses, water butts, carports, parking spaces, manhole covers and oil tanks. Particularly in a small garden, where space is very precious, a good solution is to build these utilitarian features into an attractive design from the outset.

A different approach is to screen the problem. A garden shed might be sited at the bottom of the garden, totally concealed under a mass of ivy. Telegraph poles may be screened by growing trees in the foreground. Oil tanks become less obtrusive if they are painted in a garden-toning dark finish and hidden away behind hedging or a climber-covered trellis. A compost heap (opposite far right) has a yellow brick wall behind it with handsome detailing and decoration; a rabbit hutch can be a pleasing lawn feature (see pp. 112-113); and sheds or carports (opposite below left) can be built to blend in with the garden.

Planning parking areas

Cars and car-parking spaces need careful planning. Clever detailing of the paving to provide a footpath up to the house, flanked by gravel parking spaces either side, will give the appearance of an attractive front courtyard when empty. Light trellis structures covered with climbers are also attractive and effective ways to screen and shade cars (or indeed caravans), making them less intrusive in the garden.

Concealing manhole covers

Manhole covers often crop up in unwelcome places. If you are lucky enough to choose where they should go, try to incorporate them in a border or path. They become eyesores when their siting looks haphazard. In borders, plants can be grown over them to screen them, and in paths they can be totally concealed by using recessed covers topped by matching paving.

Ideas for sheds

Before opting for a purpose-built shed that you will probably want to screen, it may make sense to design and build your own version that satisfies a need for storage but also complements the garden.

If you do not have space for a shed, choose well-designed tools and hang them high near the back door, ready for action.

This garden building forms a covered eating area during the summer when the canvas blind is rolled up. In the winter, when the blinds are down, it is used to store firewood. Designed by Honor Gibbs.

This rustic screen is interesting, provides an ideal support for climbers and at the same time shifts the eye away from the dustbin area behind it. Designed and built by Roger Storr.

In a small garden it is well worth making facilities such as compost heaps look good, maximizing on every square inch of your plot. Designed and built by Roger Storr.

This looks totally unlike a carport, and yet is one. The gravel defines where the cars go and the paving slabs take you to the door. Abundant well-designed and maintained planting show the house off at its best. Designed and constructed by Sheila and Roger Storr.

A MODERN TOWN GARDEN

When space is limited, some of the more practical items of garden living, such as manufactured paddling pools, garden sheds and rabbit hutches, need careful siting. This design offers solutions for hiding the negative and accentuating the positive in a garden. Although designed to be of interest to the whole family, this garden is particularly geared towards young children.

The play area

The garden is very open and visible from much of the house, so the play area is tucked behind a dense evergreen hedge. This allows the children to play in privacy while being sufficiently close to the house to allow some degree of supervision. It also keeps plastic play equipment out of view.

A variable width of vigorous planting surrounds two sides of this area, forming a buffer zone of tough shrubs, such as willow, bamboo and buddleia, in which the children can play. Plants such as foxgloves, ox-eye daisies and verbascum self-seed freely, providing dots of colour. At one end of the play area, a large climbing frame is well sited with plenty of surrounding space, while at the other end there is a swing.

The terrace

The terrace is the main eating and entertaining area of the garden and is a focal point for the adult part of the garden. At its widest, it is 6.5m (19ft), and it is raised 150mm (6in) above ground level so that the edge forms useful extra seating. The brick trim around the edge of the terrace provides an effective visual link with the brick of the house.

The lawn

The lawn is subject to heavy use so, to keep it looking presentable, it has been edged with a brick trim. This also helps to define and accentuate the strong curves of its shape and, again, creates a visual link with the house and terrace.

The dense evergreen hedge that frames part of the lawn forms a suitable, thick green 'net' for lobbing tennis balls back and forth, and is sturdy enough not to suffer in the process. Ball games are encouraged in the dormant season only.

A woodland boundary

At the far end of the garden, there is a narrow 3m (9ft) strip devoted to a woodland habitat. This small, wild area is also home to a garden shed, compost heap, rabbit hutch and sand pit. The pathway, created with paving slabs set into the grass, is surrounded by tough planting, and is used for chase and hide-and-seek.

This swing is sited at the end of a series of three archways highlighting a diagonal axis across the garden.

From the terrace, the first archway frames the view out to the garden and the swing at the end.

A bubble fountain is a simple, safe and attractive water feature for a family garden.

KEY

1 Bubble fountain
2 Sand pit
3 Woodland edge
4 Play area
5 Terrace
6 Dense evergreen hedge
7 Climbing frame
8 Swing/pergola
9 Pets' corner
10 Tough plant border

A SMALL CITY GARDEN

This small garden (13.5m/44ft at its longest) was designed for a couple with two young daughters. They wanted a garden that they could use for entertaining but that would also provide plenty to interest the whole family. As the garden is highly visible from the house, the views needed to be interesting throughout the year.

A raised terrace with a bold pattern of brick and paving and wide steps spilling onto the lawn forms the main eating and entertaining area. It also includes a built-in sand pit with raised brick walls. The numerous pots filling this terrace area can be rearranged seasonally, ensuring that the views from the house are always especially colourful near the building.

The main focal point of the garden is the small building that sits over the informal pool. Wide timber stepping stones lead across and up to another, narrower, paved area that is raised above the water. There is an underwater safety grid just below the surface of the pool. The maximum depth is 600mm (2ft), which does not pose a safety threat when the children are competent swimmers, at which stage the guard can be removed. Aquatic and marginal plants grow in the water, and dragonflies, newts, frogs and birds provide wildlife interest.

A climber-clad wooden pergola leads around the end of the pool and up to the raised terrace. Under the pergola, a canvas playhouse has been made by using the wooden beam of the pergola as the ridge support and driving two long wooden pegs into the wall to form side supports. The walls and roof are of heavy canvas, with a door and windows cut out.

The planting

Apart from on the terrace and the area around the water, the planting is predominantly composed of blue or white flowering species, with some purple foliage plants. Tough plants are positioned on the border edges, such as hebes and buddleias. In the summer, several large pots of brilliant blue Agapanthus are placed in any available gaps in the borders, heightening the effect of the blue-and-white colour scheme that ties the garden together in a bold but simple fashion.

This is the main eating area next to the house. Even in a small garden it is well worth making it a generous-sized space.

This brick sand pit is conveniently sited so that the children can be watched from the kitchen window.

KEY

1 Sitting area
2 Swing seat
3 Timber stepping stone
4 Pergola
5 Sand pit
6 Small sitting area
7 Pool
8 Summerhouse on stilts
9 Canvas playhouse

A Country Garden

This is a low-maintenance, high-interest garden suitable for a family with older children and teenagers. The large garden area allows room for a number of features, including an extensive terrace, pool and herb and vegetable gardens.

The front garden

Visitors approach the house from a drive, flanked on one side by a high coniferous hedge that, prior to redesign, dominated the whole front garden. By reducing the height of the coniferous hedge by a third and planting a line of deciduous trees in front of it, the oppressive impact of the massive green hedge was dispelled. The planting was kept to small, formal, box-edged beds filled with English roses, topiary and trouble-free herbaceous plants.

The terrace

At the back of the house, a paved terrace is used for barbecues, entertaining and relaxation. As the house is tucked into a slope, it worked best to divide the terrace into four different levels, each separated by steps that provide extra seating.

Water feature

The circular pool, partially surrounded by a bog garden, provides much interest. Because the house sits in a dip with the garden sloping towards it, the pool is situated almost 1m (3ft) higher than the terrace, making it a prominent feature when viewed from the house and terrace.

The orchard and pergola

At the south side of the lawn, an archway through the high hedge leads to an orchard. Here, a mown path runs through longer grass and wild flowers to a tree house, where the children have their own hide-away. This wild area is largely the children's domain and is separated from the vegetable garden by a climbing pergola (see pp. 52–53).

The vegetable garden

As the vegetable garden can be seen from the terrace, there is an emphasis on the attractive perennial crops, such as globe artichokes, rhubarb and seakale. It has a sunny site near to the kitchen and is divided into four small, easy-to-work beds.

The paved terrace runs the length of the house but is divided into four areas, separated by generous steps.

In front of the house, box-edged beds are arranged in a simple pattern and surrounded by gravel.

KEY

1 Low conifer hedge
2 Herb garden
3 Terrace
4 Circular pool
5 Bog garden
6 Archway
7 Play pergola
8 Vegetable garden
9 Tree house
10 Football goal posts

Wide stone steps lead up from the terrace to this large, circular pool. Water plants are grown in baskets, giving more control over planting.

PLAYHOUSES AND TREE HOUSES

A playhouse or tree house provides a wonderful base for recreation for children and adults, offering a private refuge quite separate from the house. Honey pots such as these are ideal for younger children, who will tend to focus their activities around them, easing the pressure on other parts of the garden. An added bonus is that they can be a visual delight as well.

THE MAGIC OF PLAYHOUSES

In today's theme-led world, manufactured playhouses may range from pirate ships to fairy-tale castles, but the more traditional designs owe much to the original 'Wendy house' as featured in the stage production of J.M. Barrie's *Peter Pan*, published in 1904. In the story, Peter asks Wendy what her dream house would be and she describes a tiny woodland house 'with funny red walls and a roof of mossy green'. Peter and the Lost Boys rapidly construct a playhouse to this design and Wendy's dream comes true.

A world of make-believe

For generations, children of the British royal family enjoyed playhouses that were really fully-equipped miniature houses, such as the Swiss Cottage at Osborne. But for complete sophistication, Queen Elizabeth II's miniature thatched cottage, given to her on her sixth birthday, is hard to better. The house not only has a bedroom, bathroom, sitting room and kitchen but also electricity, gas, hot and cold running water and sheets embroidered with the royal crest.

Fortunately, most children are pleased with much simpler structures. Much of the delight of a playhouse focuses around mimicking adult activities, and if the playhouse is quite simple it will be a springboard for a whole range of imaginative games. Above all, a playhouse is a private place to which a child can escape throughout the year. It is an especially valuable outdoor play structure becoming particularly magical when the rain beats down on the roof.

Careful siting of a playhouse is very important if one is to retain the character of the garden and provide the children with ample opportunity to play with some degree of privacy. If possible, position the house in a quiet corner or leafy glade. The foliage will both add to the fairy-tale atmosphere and diminish the presence of the structure. If you have the space, add on a small garden for vegetables and flowers (see pp. 120–122). A low fence, gate or archway will provide a structure for climbers and further define the children's territory.

Making use of a dip in the garden, this den makes a great alternative playhouse, being partially sunken, with a ladder leading down in to a well-secluded spot.

Choosing a design

The first important decision is whether to purchase a manufactured playhouse or make one yourself. Off-the-shelf playhouses come in an enormous range of styles and sizes, from wooden structures in elaborate Georgian style with many rooms, through to simple plastic boxes. The play value of smaller ones is fairly limited, so a teepee made out of beech branches may prove just as rewarding at a fraction of the price. The entertainment value to be derived from larger off-the-peg models, however, particularly ones that incorporate some form of climbing structure, may sustain your children through to their early teens.

If you decide to make your own playhouse, there is greater scope for creating a style that suits the mood of your garden. It need not entail elaborate woodwork: a few rustic poles clad with dense trellis and gaps cut for windows would provide a much-loved place for adventure, as would a willow house (see pp. 32–33). A space-saving idea is to divide a playhouse in half with a partitioning wall to provide garden storage on one side and a play area on the other.

Provided the house is constructed strictly according to instructions and that you buy off-the-shelf playhouses from accredited manufacturers, there are few dangers from this sort of play structure. Even the safest items of play equipment require a level of adult supervision appropriate to the age of the users. A hinged door may be a hazard for young children; fingers may get trapped, or some members of the group may get stuck either inside or out. The solution is either to leave the house without a door or else to supervise play.

This fine playhouse forms an exciting yet safe play area for young children. The two-storey design maximizes space while providing an excellent lookout post.

A manufactured playhouse has been given personal touches with the addition of window boxes and planting.

PROJECT: A WENDY HOUSE

This is a flexible design that can be adapted according to taste. The shutters may be cut into a different shape; the external paintwork can be changed or abandoned in favour of wood stains; and a number of extra features may be added including a house nameplate, shelves, hooks, furniture, window boxes and a small fenced garden.

You will need

- Paving slabs: eight for the base, 600 x 600mm (24 x 24in); four slabs 900 x 600mm (36 x 24in); and aggregate, sand and mortar with which to lay them
- Six sheets of 19mm (¾in) thick, exterior-grade plywood (WBP), 1220 x 2440mm (48 x 96in), 2 complete sheets for roof panels, remainder cut to the following sizes: front and back panels 2360 x 1220mm (93 x 48in); two sides 1825 x 1220mm (71¾ x 48in), reserving the two smaller rectangles left over
- Four wooden battens (**A**), 38 x 38 x 1140mm (1½ x 1½ x 44¾in)
- Two wooden battens (**B**), 38 x 38 x 2240mm (1½ x 1½ x 88¼in)
- One wooden ridge beam (**C**), 19 x 75 x 2440mm (¾ x 3 x 96in)
- Two wooden strips (**D**), 19 x 75 x 1625mm (¾ x 3 x 96in)
- Two wooden strips (**E**), 19 x 75 x 490mm (¾ x 3 x 19¼in)
- Two wooden strips (**F**), 19 x 100 x 2440mm (¾ x 4 x 96in)
- All timber (excluding plywood) to be planed all round (PAR), tanalized softwood
- Wire nails, 32mm (1¼in) long
- Screws, No. 8, countersunk 32mm (1¼in) long
- Screws, No. 8, countersunk 38mm (1½in) long

- Weatherproof wood glue
- Two 305mm (12in) T-hinges for door, black japanned
- Door knob
- Magnetic door closer
- Fourteen 102mm (4in) T-hinges for shutters, black japanned (for front and one end panel)
- Eleven gate hooks and eyes with screw ends as shutter catches, galvanized
- Primer, undercoat and gloss paint

Tools
- Power jigsaw • Tenon saw
- Drill, power or hand • Drill bits for No. 8 screws • Countersinker • Screwdriver, power or hand • Hammer

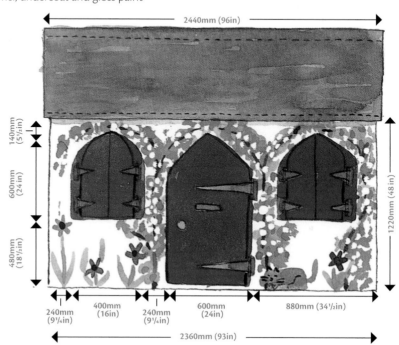

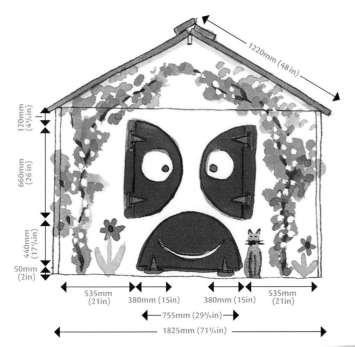

1220mm (48 in)

120mm (4¾in)

660mm (26in)

440mm (17¼in)

50mm (2in)

535mm (21in) **380mm (15in)** **380mm (15in)** **535mm (21in)**

755mm (29¾in)

1825mm (71¼in)

window opening, 400 x 600mm (16 x 24in). Fold this in half vertically and mark out half the outline of the shutter so that, once you have cut it out, the unfolded sheet provides a symmetrical template. Use a straight edge to mark the straight lines and a flexi-curve or similar to provide the arch required. Using the template, draw around the shutter and door outlines on to the front panel.

4 Cut out the door and shutters. Care is needed in sawing out. The easiest way to start is by drilling a hole where the hinge will cover it to hide the irregularity of the outline. With a jigsaw, saw very slowly and carefully along the marked shape. Repeat for the other shutter and door. Put aside the cut-out doors and shutters.

Getting started

1 Start with the floor. Lay the paving slabs a little larger than the floor area of the house – approximately 2.2 x 2.5m (86 x 98in). To prevent water collecting around the base of the plywood, lay the paving either to a fall of about 1:40, taking the water away from the walls, or else lay it with wide 20mm (¾in) joints filled with free-draining gravel.

Front and back panels

2 Start by marking the positions of the door and windows on the front panel. Fix the four wooden battens (A) to the backs of the front and back panels, parallel to the short end of the sheet and 20mm (¾in) away from it. Position the battens 30mm (1¼in) from the bottom and 50mm (2in) from the top. Mark the position of the battens on the inside of the panels first. Drill clearance holes for No. 8 wood screws centrally between the marked lines at 300mm (12in) centres. Countersink

the holes on the outside face of the panels so that the screw heads will be recessed and can be filled later. Drill pilot holes through the clearance holes into the battens. Then coat the battens with glue on one side and clamp them on to the panels before, finally, fixing them with wood screws.

3 Proceed next with the door and shutters on the front panel. In the illustration, an alternative design has been shown for the side shutters. Select the preferred design and make a cardboard template. For the gothic shutters, use a sheet of card the size of the

Side panels

5 The two side panels are made up from a rectangle fixed to an isosceles triangle, which is made up of two triangles cut from the board remaining after the side panels have been cut. The lengths of the triangle sides are 610m (24in) and 932mm (36⅝in), with a right angle as shown. To fix the two triangles together, glue and screw them along their shorter sides with a strip of wood (E), set 38mm (1½in) from the longer edges. Then fix the joined triangles onto the side panel

with the strip of wood (D), again glued and screwed with 30mm (1¼in) screws at about 300mm (12in) centres. Prepare both side panels in this way.

6 Decide on the design of the side shutters and make a template; mark this out on the plywood sheet accordingly and carefully saw out as for the front panel in Step 4. Cut a 75 x 19mm (3 x ¾in) notch out of the apex of the two side panels to take the ridge beam.

Fixing the panels together

7 Now comes the fun part, when the Wendy house starts to take shape. Stand the back panel upright, lean it against something or, better still, ask someone to support it. Stand up the back panel and one of the side panels (with the gable end attached) and, making sure that bottom edges are flush, drill and

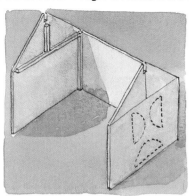

screw the edge of the side panel to the batten behind the back panel, using the 38mm (1¼in) screws – do not glue. These two sides will now be self-supporting, so it is an easy matter to fix the other end panel in the same manner. The front can now be fixed in a similar fashion.

The roof

8 Slot the ridge beam (C) into the apex of the gables and nail it to the edge of the panels with two round-headed nails, 32mm (1¼in) long, at each end.

9 Fix a wooden batten (B) to each full sheet of plywood for the roof panels; position it centrally on the length, parallel to one long edge with the far side of the batten 1059mm (41⅝in) from that edge. This measurement must be accurate so that the roof panels butt up tightly. Again use glue and 38mm (1½in) screws at about 300mm (12in) centres. Repeat with the other full sheet.

10 You will now need a strong person to help you. Lift the first of the roofing panels, resting the batten that has been fixed to its lower underside against the top of the back panel. Lower the roofing panel slowly on to the ridge beam, making sure that it overlaps the gable ends equally on either side before

nailing it to the panel edges and the ridge beam. This process will correct any skewing of the side panels when they were fixed to the front and back panels, although it may be better to loosen the screws while the roofing panel is positioned. Repeat the lowering and fixing procedure with the second roofing panel.

11 In order to protect the gap at the apex of the roof, screw two strips of timber (F) over the middle joint, using 32mm (1¼in) screws, with one overlapping the edge of the other.

Finishing door and shutters

12 Cut the shutters in half vertically, if using the gothic design. Screw on the hinges and fix the shutters to the house. It may be necessary to chamfer the inside edge of each shutter to facilitate opening and closing. Screw gate hooks and eye catches to shutters and walls so shutters may be held open and closed (use three gate hooks and eye catches per pair of shutters). Screw the hinges on to the door, then fix the door on to the house (see p27); fit a door knob and a magnetic closer. If you wish to paint the exterior, prime and undercoat, then gloss the walls, door and shutters with the chosen colour. Alternatively, finish with a wood stain.

ALTERNATIVE PLAYHOUSES

Children appreciate small, personalized spaces that they adapt to suit their current interests. Rather than providing a ready-made playhouse, alternative play spaces, such as dens and willow houses, will stimulate their imaginations and often blend in well with the rest of the garden. Dens can be made in so many ways from so many different materials that it makes sense to build them around features that are readily available to you.

A tent appeals to all ages. Use boldly striped fabrics to clad a well-proportioned frame for a striking den that has lots of imaginative play potential.

Willow houses are very satisfying to make as they are simple, inexpensive and fun. Willows are well known for the ease with which most of them root from leafless cuttings or even from stems several years old. The vigorous varieties will even root from lengths as long as 2.4–3.6m (8–12ft). The other helpful factor is their rapid growth rate, which ensures that your willow tunnel, tepee or igloo will, in good conditions, be covered with a curtain of greenery in the first season.

The addition of a tunnel to a willow teepee greatly enhances its play value. By allocating this sort of play space to your children to shape as they please, you will be providing great opportunities for creative play that will often centre around building and 'improving' the space as much as playing in it.

Made from sturdy beech branches bound at the top, this den provides an ideal framework for climbing plants. Older children will enjoy the challenge of planning and constructing a den like this.

PROJECT: A CROCODILE WILLOW HOUSE

The main ingredient needed for this splendid crocodile is a copious supply of long willow cuttings. The varieties of *Salix* best suited to this structure are *Salix triandra* (almond-leafed willow) and *Salix viminalis* (common osier). Several other larger shrub or small tree willows will do, but avoid *Salix caprea* (goat willow), which does not sprout so well, and *Salix fragilis* (crack willow), which, as the name suggests, is brittle and much less pliable than the recommended species.

Preparation

1 Between autumn and spring, on clean soil free of perennial weeds, mark out your crocodile on the ground. Then dig a narrow trench, 100mm (4in) wide and 150mm (6in) deep around the outline. Incorporate some free-draining grit into the back-fill if possible. Take cuttings of the required length, depending on the proportions of your crocodile. These cuttings are best taken immediately below a leaf axil. If you have difficulty finding long cuttings, take two (or even three) cuttings and bind them where they overlap. Push the cuttings into the trench bottom as securely as possible. Back-fill the trench.

2 Weave cut branches around the sides to form instant 'walls', leaving gaps for eyes and entrance doorways as required. Graduate the length of the cuttings to get the desired curvaceous effect, making the tummy large enough for your children to fit into. Water the crocodile until established.

3 As 'planted' shoots sprout, weave in the living shoots to make the crocodile grow. Plant small thicker stub cuttings to make feet. Maintain by weaving in the new growths.

CHOOSING A TREE HOUSE

Tree houses, or 'roosting places' as they were called in Tudor England, are one of the most exhilarating places in which children may play. They form a 'nest' perched up high among rustling leaves, giving children a secret vantage point from which to survey the rest of the garden. Today they are regaining their popularity, and deservedly so, particularly in small gardens where it can be difficult to accommodate a ground-level building successfully. By siting the building above eye level, partially camouflaged by branches and leaves, it is much less dominant and blends easily with its surroundings.

With a little imagination and ingenuity, tree houses can become complete play centres.

Design considerations

The essential ingredient of any good tree house is, of course, a suitable tree; its height and structure will to some extent dictate the tree house design. As you will see on the following pages, it is not necessary to have a tree with a wide, branching limb structure. In fact, a tree house can be partially or entirely free-standing. It may be in the tree, by the tree, or even slung between trees.

For children between five and ten years old, an old apple tree often provides suitable branches for a tree house. Ideally, the platform should be just 1m (3ft) off the ground and should have a secure balustrade, a minimum height of 750mm (30in), with the gaps between the railings no larger than 100mm (4in). The design of the access is particularly important as this is where most accidents happen, with children pushing and racing to get up or down first. To be really safe, make a staircase to the tree house; otherwise position a fixed ladder with a bannister at an angle of about 60°. The ladder should have rounded rungs 25–38mm (1–1½in) in diameter, so that children's hands can get a good grip. The treads or rungs should not be too close together or they may trap small feet.

The soil around the base of a tree dries out quickly and can become as hard as concrete. It is a good idea to make a soft landing below the ladder, by providing an area of sand, gravel or bark (see pp. 46–47). Young children will need close supervision until their agility is sufficiently developed. If you also have very young children that you want to bar from the tree house, make the access selective by positioning the first rung well out of reach, or have a removable ladder.

Elaborate or simple?

A tree house fulfils a child's need for excitement and fantasy while also providing them with a quiet place of their own. From an aesthetic point of view, they also blend into a garden, often adding a magical element that has great charm. If you have the space, add extra features to the tree house, such as rope ladders, scramble nets or a trapeze, and it will soon become your children's main focus for play outside.

Alternatively, you may want to design a tree house that all the family can enjoy. A rustic design with a pitched roof may be appropriate in some gardens, the roof being either thatched or tiled with wooden shingles. For a more sophisticated look, the walls could be made from plywood, allowing elaborately shaped doors and windows in the Gothic or Tudor style. The finish could be rendered or painted with a green or brown stain, or even with Tuscan pink (see p. 38). If there is the space, a balcony looking out on the garden is a real luxury.

For those who find the prospect of building a tree house too daunting but would like a design that is individual, there are several firms that specialize in making them (see page 128). Your local tree surgeon may also be able to put you in touch with a suitable firm.

This tree house is specifically for younger children. The totally enclosed sides make falling out unlikely and there is a small window in one end providing views out. The access points often provide scope for accidents, so here a sturdy ladder has been chosen instead of a rope ladder. A hand rail would make the ladder safer still.

This is a real home in the trees. It was made from a converted dog kennel fixed between two tall pine trees. The balcony, although narrow, adds another dimension and enables children to have high-level picnics outside in the sunshine.

This tree and tree house provide many movable features to encourage agility as well as offer amusement. As the tree house is mainly above eye level it has less visual impact on the garden than a ground-level climbing frame, for example.

PLANNING A TREE HOUSE

Ideally, the tree you choose should be healthy, with no signs of rot or decay, no pockets of water collecting in it, and no dead wood in the canopy. Avoid species that tend to shed branches, such as horse chestnut and *Robinia pseudoacacia* (false acacia), and for preference choose an oak or an old orchard tree, especially an apple or pear (but not plum).

It is often recommended that the tree should be mature, as building a structure in a rapidly growing young tree may well hinder its natural development. However, if you have an otherwise suitable semi-mature tree in your garden do not necessarily rule it out; just bear in mind that the structure must be able to stand up to the tree's growth without too much distortion, and the tree must be able to expand without being impeded.

A suitable tree

The shape and height of the tree is crucial. A tree with spreading branches will probably not be able to accommodate a platform of useful size without the removal of one or two limbs. If the tree has a preservation order on it or is in a conservation area, permission from your local planning authority will be required to put a structure in it, and to carry out tree surgery. Otherwise much depends on the structure of the tree house and the interpretation of the planning legislation. If the structure is only a few planks lashed to a tree and is meant to be temporary, a planning authority is unlikely to get involved. In the UK, however, if the cubic capacity is greater than 10 cubic metres (30 cubic feet), if it is higher than 4m (12ft) [or 3m (9ft) if it has a flat roof], or if it is near a highway or overlooking another dwelling, then it is worth seeking further advice.

It is not safe to build a tree house out on a single branch. If this position is the only possible one, rest the structure on the branch and add a sturdy framework around it to make the house self-supporting. As the tree grows, make sure that the supporting framework is still secure and is not being pulled out of the ground.

A self-supporting structure in a tree is often the simplest form of tree house, requiring only minimal damage to the tree. However, if your garden has no suitable trees you can build a house on stilts, with climbers planted to grow up them. Plant three or four young trees (1.2–1.5m/4–5ft high), without stakes, and train the branches around the house. Choose fast-growing trees, for example *Prunus avium* (wild cherry) or *Sorbus aucuparia* (mountain ash) for small gardens. Always remember to check that the force of the growth of the trees is not making the structure unstable.

This tree house has been designed as a dynamic play structure with movable features such as ladders and ropes.

Construction

The best method of fixing the structure to the tree is debatable. One arboriculturist of some note has stated that lashing the structure to the tree with man-made rope, as is often recommended, can cause considerable damage, as tree houses are liable to be forgotten about when the children have passed a certain age. It is believed that the occasional screw fixing into the tree will do less damage.

A heavy-duty pallet makes an ideal platform, but you must shape or pad the edges where it fits in the tree to prevent scarring. If you make your own platform it is better to use softwood rather than hardwood, partly because it is cheaper and lighter but also because if it is forgotten about in years to come it will do less damage to the tree.

When you are planning how to construct the tree house, aim to make it as light as possible. Exterior-grade ply is ideal for the walls and for the roof, though the latter could be made from treated hardboard or canvas, which would be lighter still. Do not forget that safety is paramount, and the house and tree need to be checked over at least twice a year.

The solid walls, with just a small window and roof, make this tree house safe for young children.

If you are lucky enough to have a tree with widespread limbs that enable you to build an unsupported tree house, make the most of it.

Placing a tree house between two or more trunks can be very effective. However, when the wind blows the house will move between the supporting trees.

A tree house resting out on a limb is not structurally safe unless you provide it with additional supporting posts, as illustrated here.

Building the tree house around the trunk is an excellent way to anchor your structure. Additional load-bearing posts will provide much of the support.

Tree house variations

Built as a treetop office, complete with computer and fax machine, this tree house has a 2m (6ft 6in) square room inside. A balcony provides a small, enchanting area in which to work outside and leads to a high walkway that provides access in a less precipitous form than the ladder. The Tuscan pink render and verdigris paint finish are new but have been hand-mixed and distressed to give a weathered look. For paint finishes, it is well worth a little time, trouble and experimentation to achieve an out-of-the-ordinary colour.

This high-level tree house in a mature willow provides a vantage point over water meadows. It is built for older children, providing bags of scope for that essential exhilaration factor. The house has been designed to grow with the family, with plans to develop an additional storey.

A hollow tree, should you have one or find one that you can move to your garden, makes a very special den. This one is a hollow, pollarded willow, converted for children's use. In A.A. Milne's *Winnie the Pooh* stories, much of the action takes place in and around hollow trees, which enhances their natural charms for children even further.

This ivy-clad tree house, which sits in an old apple tree, was designed and built by Peter Farrell. It is low level and therefore safe for use by the younger members of the family. However, it also incorporates special features, such as a balancing log linked to a climbing structure at one end, to capture the interest of slightly older children.

PROJECT: A CHILDREN'S TREE HOUSE

Few people have in their garden the ideal tree, with spreading boughs, for holding a tree house, so this one is designed to be self-supporting, with all the load on the posts. An old, mature tree can be utilized for additional support, but allow plenty of clearance for growth in younger trees. The height and accessibility of the house may be altered to suit the needs of your family, and the shape of the tree. The platform of this one is 1.8m (6ft) from the ground, and as such only older, agile children should be allowed on it without close supervision. You may need to consult your local planning authority.

Here pallets are used to form a ready-made base. These come in many different sizes, so adaptation may be necessary.

You will need

House

- One and a half heavy-duty close-boarded matching pallets, 1.2 x 1.2m and 1.2 x 0.6m (4 x 4ft and 4 x 2ft). Pallets differ, and you may have to vary – but not decrease – timber sizes accordingly
- Four 3.8m (12ft 6in) hardwood poles for main posts, 125mm (5in) in diameter
- Two 1.5m (5ft) base beams, 75 x 75mm (3 x 3in)
- Two 1.8m (6ft) crossrails, 75 x 100mm (3 x 4in), planed to fit snugly in pallet
- Two 2.7m (9ft) diagonal braces 63mm (2½in) in diameter
- Two 1.2m (4ft) end boards, 125mm x 38mm (5 x 1½in)
- One 3.2m (10ft 6in) ladder side, 75 x 75mm (3 x 3in), free of knots [see note]
- One 2.3m (7ft 6in) ladder side, 75 x 75mm (3 x 3in), free of knots
- One 870mm (34in) corner post, 85mm (3¼in) in diameter [see note]

- 5.9m (19ft 4in) length of balustrade, 63mm (2½in) in diameter
- Thirty-four 870mm (34in) spindles, 35mm (1⅜in) in diameter [see note]
- Two 1150mm (45in) battens, 50 x 50mm (2 x 2in)
- Nine 1.2m (4ft) spindle braces, 75mm (3in) in diameter [see note]
- Seven 600mm (24in) ladder rungs, 35 x 50mm (1⅜ x 2in), free of knots
- Two triangular spacers, 100 x 100 x 70 x 75mm (4 x 4 x 2¾ x 3in) thick, cut to suit
- Hardcore or coarse gravel 0.05m³ (0.07 cu.yd)
- Concrete mix 1:6 (cement:ballast), 0.5m³ (0.7 cu.yd)
- Four 225mm (9in) coach bolts with protective coating, M10 (10mm/⅜in), plus single coil and flat washers, and nuts
- Sixteen 200mm (8in) coach bolts (as above). (Lengths may vary depending on thicknesses of wood in pallet and of poles)
- Three 125mm (5in) and four 150mm (6in) wood screws

- Other common sizes of rustproof screws and nails

Roof

- Eight 500mm (20in) corner braces, 63mm (2½in) in diameter
- Two 1450mm (57in) base beams, 35 x 63mm (1⅜ x 2½in)
- Two 1120mm (44in) base beams, 35 x 63mm (1⅜ x 2½in)
- Four 1450mm (57in) rafters, 35 x 63mm (1⅜ x 2½in)
- One 110mm (4⅜in) centre block, cut from 50 x 75mm (2 x 3in) sawn wood
- 75mm (3in) dowel, 8mm (⁵⁄₁₆in) in diameter
- One ball finial, 100mm (4in) in diameter
- Two 1450mm (57in) baseboards, 200 x 19mm (8 x ¾in)
- Two 1120mm (44in) baseboards, 200 x 19mm (8 x ¾in)
- Twenty-four roof battens (varying lengths), 25 x 35mm (1 x 1½in)
- Four 1050mm (41⅜in) lengths of broom handle

- Wood offcuts or shingles, approx. 150 x 300 x 7mm (6 x 12 x ¼in)
- Rustproof screws and nails
- Waterproof woodworking adhesive
- Non-toxic wood preservative

Note: Hardwood is advisable for the poles. The remaining wood could be hardwood or pressure impregnated, PAR softwood. Lengths of balustrade timbers and long ladder side are for a 750mm (30in) high balustrade. Adjust accordingly for a 900mm (36in) height.

Tools
- Portable workbench • Steel measuring tape
- Steel rule • Spade • Shovel • Power drill
- High-speed wood drill bit • Extension rod
- Drill bits • Hammer • Screwdriver
- Try square or combination square
- Adjustable sliding bevel • Panel saw (or circular saw) • Tenon saw • Dowelling jig
- Dowel bit • Wood plane • Spanners • Chisel
- Mallet• Hacksaw • File

Building the platform

1 Take the four main posts and saw three-quarter segments out of the tops to a depth of 35mm (1½in). The four corners of the roof base timbers will sit in these recesses.

Having decided on the exact position and height of the tree house, dig four holes 450 x 450 x 700mm (18 x 18 x 28in) deep in a rectangle, with 1200mm (48in) between the posts on the long sides and 875mm (34½in) between those on the short sides. Put a 50mm (2in) layer of free-draining hardcore or coarse gravel into the base of each hole and ram down. Brace the posts vertically in the holes, ensuring the tops are correctly positioned to take the roof, and that the spacings are correct for the pallets.

2 Fill the holes with concrete to within 50mm (2in) of the surface. Slope the concrete surface away from the posts to shed water. Check the position of the posts again. When the concrete has set (about 48–72 hours), position the base beams at a height of 1.7m (5ft 8in), or to suit,

across the front and back posts. Fix the beams to the posts with 225mm (9in) coach bolts. Where the base beams cross the posts, flatten the round posts by removing about 20mm (¾in) with a chisel so the interface is flat on both surfaces.

3 Lay the pallet on the base beams, front midway across the front beam. Drill holes for coach bolts through each post into the pallet side timbers. Insert the cross rails, one end flush with the back of the pallet, and

move the pallet forward so you can continue the holes into the cross rails. Remove the rails and enlarge the holes to fit over the nuts and washers that will secure the pallet to the posts. Reposition the pallet and bolt to the posts.

4 Replace the cross rails inside the pallet and secure them with one screw through the top of each slat and three screws through each of the pallet side beams. Secure the half-pallet in the same way.

5 To strengthen the protruding half-pallet (the balcony), run two diagonal braces from the bases of the rear posts against the front posts to the sides of the front pallet; they should finish 85mm (3½in) back from the front edge of the pallet to allow for fixing the corner post and long ladder side. Where the diagonal braces meet the posts and pallet, flatten the rounded surfaces by about 20mm

(¾in). Fix them to the posts and pallet sides with the 200mm (8in) coach bolts. The braces will have to bend inwards to the pallet sides. If they will not flex, use a block of wood as a spacer to fill the gap and increase the bolt length.

6 Fix the end boards over the front and back ends of the platform, with three screws into the end of each of the four pallet rails.

Building the roof

7 The roof base beams will lie flat in the recesses cut in the main posts. Assemble them with glue and two screws per joint. Cut a halving (lap) joint at each end of the roof base timbers to join them together. Use the template to mark the end of the 50 x 75mm (2 x 3in) centre block to connect the rafters. Lie the rectangle flat, pin string lines along the diagonals, then lay the rafters on edge centrally along the string lines; prop them in the centre on an offcut of base beam with a piece of card on top. This will be used to make a template for the roof centre block. Opposing ends of the rafters should be 50mm (2in) apart. Mark across the ends of the rafters on to the card and complete the hexagon so formed. Cut the block to shape and plane the cut faces. Drill a central hole 25mm (1in) deep for the finial

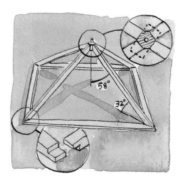

dowel and glue in the dowel. Cut the bottom ends of the rafters at 32° to the upper face and the top ends at 58°.

8 With help, hold up the rafters against the centre block so it is flush at the bottom. Glue and screw the rafter bottom ends to the base beams, with the ends flush with the corners of the rectangle, and the top ends to the centre block. Fix battens to the rafters on one surface of the roof at a time, and cut the

ends at an angle along the centre line of the rafters. Nail the first batten on edge at the bottom of the rafters. Fix the next one flat and parallel to it, 75mm (3in) up the rafters; nail subsequent battens flat and spaced 145mm (5¾in) apart. Screw the baseboards to the bottom two battens, overhanging at the bottom by 50mm (2in); angle the ends as for the battens.

9 Nail wood offcuts or shingles to the roof battens, working from the bottom upwards, so that the vertical joints are staggered 75mm (3in) in adjacent rows and each row overlaps the one below by about half its length. Cut the shingles along the line of the rafters at the end rows. Nail the top triangular pieces to the projecting centre block. Screw lengths of broom handle to the rafters, then fit the finial.

10 Lift the completed roof into position on the pre-shaped ends of the main posts so that the roof base timbers rest in the recesses. (This is a job for at least three people.) Drill two holes up at an angle in each post; screw through these into the base beams.

11 Screw the corner braces to the base beams and posts. Notch the long ladder side over the pallet with a bird's-mouth joint then cut a triangular spacer to fill the gap. Screw through the ladder side and spacer into the pallet. Flatten the corner post at one end and fix it to the front left side of the pallet with three 125mm (5in) screws. Screw the long ladder side to the front right side.

Erecting the balustrade and ladder

12 Run the balustrade outside the posts, with a gap for access. It should be at least 750mm (30in) high (900mm/36in for larger children). Notch the main posts 20mm (¾in) deep where it crosses them and mitre the balustrade corners. Bolt to the main posts, corner post and long ladder side with 200mm (8in) coach bolts and skew nail the corners together.

13 Screw spindles to the inside of the balustrade and the sides of the base, at a

General tips

- Cut off protruding bolt ends with a hacksaw and file them flush. Treat all timber with two coats of preservative.
- Plant climbers against the posts, avoiding the concrete. Suitable shade-loving plants would be honeysuckle such as *Lonicera japonica* 'Halliana', and/or ivy such as *Hedera colchica* 'Dentata'. Water frequently, as the roots will be competing with those of the tree.
- Check every six months for signs of rot, damage or loose fixings, and check that the tree remains healthy and safe.

maximum of 100mm (4in) apart. At front and back, where the base projects beyond the balustrade, fix the bottom ends to 50 x 50mm (2 x 2in) battens screwed across the pallets if the spindles don't curve enough to allow fixing to the sides. Add V-braces for extra strength; their length will depend on their position. Screw the V-shaped braces, angled at the ends, to the underside of the balustrade and to the base or battens. Fit an extra brace from the top of the corner post on the long side.

14 Place the shorter ladder side firmly in position, parallel to the long ladder side, and secure it to the pallet over a triangular spacer. Cut it flush with the top of the pallet. Round off the top edge of the rungs and screw to the ladder sides, spaced about 250mm (10in) apart.

This tree house, hidden amid the ivy, quickly into its surroundings to provide a natural hideaway at the bottom of the garden.

GARDEN GAMES

With more space, more freedom and the stimulation of the outdoor environment, the garden offers a more enticing area for play than the house. There is great scope for providing a wide range of energetic activities, from exhilarating cable runways to simple rope swings, while some action-filled games require no more than a ball and an expanse of lawn.

PLAY AREAS

For children to make the most of play areas, they should be exciting yet safe. The environment should capture their imagination, stimulate and entice them. Consider the age range of the children, the funds, the size of the garden and what the children enjoy best. Site the equipment so that you can provide the required level of supervision.

A swing structure can be relatively simple to make (see pp. 48–49) and, by changing the seats from cradle seats to flat seats, you can adapt it as the children grow. The swing's harmless appearance belies the fact that it is also the source of many accidents. See opposite for safety considerations.

Ready-made climbing frames are not always the easiest items to blend into the garden, but exciting designs can be found made of wood (see pp. 52–53). Always provide a safe landing surface of bark, sand or gravel. Simple wooden balancing bars, a series of log stepping stones and horizontal

Children may not always use play areas as originally intended, pushing every piece of equipment to the limit. Remove the equipment if the children have grown too old for its proper use or point out the dangers. Bear in mind, too, that a group of raucous children will embark upon hazardous play they would think twice about in more sober moments. Also, bear in mind that the tolerance and loading of most equipment does not usually allow for the large numbers that may be present at birthday parties.

bars of different heights are also easy to make and entertaining.

A cable runway comprises a rope suspended from two points with a pulley and a button seat. Ensure the area that the traveller passes through is totally unobstructed.

If there is a suitable slope, slides are relatively easy to accommodate. If not, you will need the free-standing sort that do not blend easily into the average-sized garden.

Playing safe

Position two or more pieces of equipment so that the likelihood of collisions is minimized. Any structure, whether home-made or not, must be thoroughly checked a minimum of three times a year for signs of rotting timbers, frayed ropes, movement of joints and so on, and any problems dealt with accordingly.

Swing safety
Children tend to swing higher and higher and when someone crosses their path they are unable to prevent a collision. Site the swing away from popular routes and do not let toddlers run around unchecked. Purchase a flat rubber safety seat, as wooden swing seats rarely have impact-absorbing edges and plastic seats can splinter on impact. Old tyres are also not recommended as they contain steel reinforcing wires.

Climbing safety
Building a climbing frame to your own design requires careful thought. It must be stable and capable of taking occasional, larger loads. In addition, the design must avoid finger traps and head traps, the ladder rungs should be the right shape and size for children's hands to grip, and the timber should be planed rather than sawn to avoid splinters and pressure-treated with preserva-

tive. The structure should also be bolted and screwed, rather than nailed together. Ensure that the height and scale of the frame is appropriate to the age of the children.

When you are constructing or mending items, avoid using nails. Use stainless steel or good-quality zinc-plated fixings. Cut off and file smooth protruding bolt ends and paint the ends with a zinc-rich paint.

Laying a safety surface
If you provide a safety surface under equipment you will reduce the severity of any accidents. It is best to sink the safety surface so that it is flush with the ground. However, in poorly drained ground, raise the surface above ground level or put in drainage.

A swing is a perennial favourite, enjoyed in all weathers and by all ages. Hung under established trees, swings make an attractive garden feature in themselves.

Bark
• Has excellent impact-absorbing qualities (better than sand or gravel) and is easy to install.
• Ideally it should be laid to a depth of 300mm (12in).
• The best is a granular bark that comes mainly from pine trees (*Pinus* spp.).
• Spread the bark, allow it to settle and then top it up. It will become displaced easily and will need raking.
• Check regularly that no stones have strayed into it.

Sand
• Is loved by most children for its soft, fine texture. Its drawback is that cats love it too.
• Avoid using a sharp building sand, which forms a hard, non-shock-absorbing surface.
• Sand should be laid to a depth of 300mm (12in) and will need regular raking to maintain a soft landing.

Gravel
• Is rarely used.
• The particles must be rounded rather than angular.
• The depth should be 300mm (12in) and it will need raking to maintain the depth.

Unless your ground is very well drained you should install a free-draining base of hardcore or coarse gravel to a depth of about 150mm (6in) and lay this to a fall to take the excess water away. You will probably need to edge the area to contain the surface.

PROJECT: A DOUBLE SWING

Even if you have only one child, a double swing is worth the extra effort when friends come to play. The rustic frame of this design helps it blend into the garden and tough climbers may be established to incorporate the play structure still further.

Practical tips for safety

Site the swing carefully, making sure that it is not positioned where passers-by are likely to be hit by an enthusiastic swinger. A safety surface of bark, rounded particle sand or rounded particle gravel, laid over a length of 2.5m (8ft 3in) in front of and behind the seat and to the width of the swing frame, provides a good soft landing.

Fit a rubber safety seat (see Suppliers, page 128) hung at an inside angle of 85° to prevent the seat swinging from side to side.

You will need · · · · · · · ·

- Four tanalized, peeled rustic poles, 3.85m (12ft 8in) long, 100–150mm (4–6in) in diameter, to form two pairs of 'legs'
- Two supporting side poles, 3.9m (12ft 10in) long, 100–150mm (4–6in) in diameter
- One tanalized, peeled rustic cross pole, a maximum of 3.7m (12ft 2in) long, 100–150mm (4–6in) in diameter (use the thicker dimension if the children are heavy.)
- Concrete, 1:6 mix cement: ballast, 0.75m³ (1cu.yd)
- One barrow load of free-draining granular material
- Two ready-made rubber safety swing seats,

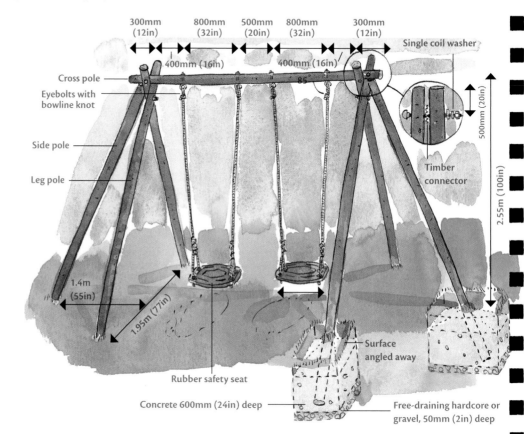

such as a belt seat that comes with metal rings to attach the rope to a flat rubber safety seat that also requires four eyebolts M10 (10mm/³⁄₈in) diameter with 25mm (1in) shank and nut or a single tier, or a rubber cradle seat, which comes with a metal ring to attach the rope to
- Synthetic rope with a breaking strength of ½ ton, approximately 12m (40ft) in length

(note that, if swing chains are used instead of ropes, they require suitable bearing assemblies to fix to eyebolts)
- Four eyebolts M10 (10mm/³⁄₈ in) diameter, with shanks 125–175mm (5–7in) long, depending on the pole thickness, the eye to be of sufficient size to take the rope
- Coach bolts with protective coating, M10 (10mm/³⁄₈ in) diameter, of length to suit

poles, with single coil washers, washers and nuts: two to join leg poles, 200–300mm (8–12in) long; four to attach cross pole, 240–340mm (9½ –13½in) long
- Two wooden connectors, size to suit poles
- Round wire nails, galvanized 150mm (6in) long

Tools
- Saw • Chisel • Spade • Shovel • Hammer
- Drill • Spanner • Plumb-line • String lines/pins

Building the swing

1 First prepare the poles for the legs. Lay each pair of leg poles on the ground in the shape of an 'X'. The poles should cross about 500mm (20in) from their tops (the thinner ends), making an angle of approximately 46°. This angle is produced by having the centre line of the poles 1.95m (77in) apart at a point measured 2.5m (98½in) down each leg from the centre point where the poles cross. Mark the area where each pole overlaps and cut this portion away to form a flat-notched face about 20mm (¾in) deep.

2 Lay the leg poles in pairs to form crosses, with their notched faces together. Support the uppermost pole at the end furthermost from the joint so that it is parallel to the ground and then drill a hole through the joint to take the coach bolt. Fix the bolt using a wooden connector between the posts, and a plain washer and a single coil washer before the nut. Tighten the nuts.

3 Mark the approximate point where the cross pole is to be bolted to the leg poles, and mark the approximate positions for the eyebolts (see illustration). Drill holes to take the eyebolts, in a straight line and through the axis of the pole; this is important to avoid weakening the cross pole. Fix the bolts using a large plain washer, then a single coil washer, before the nut.

4 Mark out the position of the four leg poles and then the two side poles. For 100mm (4in) diameter poles, dig rectangular holes, 600 x 350mm (24 x 14in); for 150mm (6in) diameter poles, extend the width of the holes to 400mm (16in). Dig the holes 850mm (34in) deep; place 50mm (2in) of free-draining hardcore or coarse gravel in the base of each hole and firm it down.

5 Stand the leg poles in the holes and stretch a string line along the centre axis of the holes on each side. Use a plumb-line to make sure that each joint is vertically above a point halfway along the axis. Support with a batten nailed temporarily in position and check along the pairs of poles that the inner 'faces' just straddle the axis (see illustration).

6 Next, lift the cross pole into place with the eyebolts hanging vertically. For security, tie the ends of the cross pole into place temporarily, then drill holes through one end of the cross pole and the upper ends of the leg poles and bolt together, with the bolt heads downwards. Repeat for the other end. Tighten the bolts, using washers and single coil washers before the nuts to stop them unfastening.

7 Making sure that the poles are central in the holes, stand one of the side poles in its hole and mark the exact position where the top face meets the underside of the cross pole. Saw off the top of the side pole at an angle of approximately 60° then prop it in the hole. Skew nail the side pole securely into the cross pole and the nearest leg pole, with 150mm (6in) galvanized round wire nails. Repeat for the other side pole.

8 Ram concrete into the holes to within 200mm (8in) of the top and smooth it so that the concrete is angled away from the poles to allow for drainage. Leave the concrete to set for 48–72 hours.

9 Fix the eyebolts and hang the swing seats at the required height. Hang the rope at an inside angle of 85° to ensure that it swings straight. Knot the rope firmly onto the eyebolt using a bowline knot (see p. 51).

10 Regularly check that the ropes are not starting to fray, that the wood is sound, that all the fixings are secure and for general wear and tear.

ALTERNATIVE PLAY FEATURES

If you do not have the space or the desire to have a conventional climbing frame in your garden, there are a number of alternative play features, such as a maze or balancing posts, which are often quite simple and inexpensive to construct. These more informal ideas are less finished and more dynamic and change and develop with the child's imagination – a rope ladder hung from a tree can be a fire engine's hoist one day and a ship's ladder the next.

A dead tree trunk can be anchored to the ground in concrete to make a rustic climbing feature, with pegs fixed into the wood (see opposite).

Mazes for all ages

Mazes provide outdoor puzzles that fascinate all ages. Low-growing mazes of dwarf hedges of hyssop, santolina, box or thyme form a delightful, often sweet-smelling, pattern that is immediately obvious. A central feature such as an arbour, seat or sundial can add a delightful element to a family garden. Laid out with tough dwarf hedges such as *Buxus sempervirens* or *Hebe anomala* and with a narrow path of gravel edged with brick, it can be used for gentle strolling or for games of chase.

Alternatively, if you have a small patch of garden going spare, a more rugged maze could form the centrepiece for children's activities in a wilder part of the garden. The basic network can be cut out of the turf, and different attractions can be sited in 'lay-bys' off the paths: a sunken sand pit, a mounded area to make a miniature amphitheatre, a small weeping tree for a hideaway, stepping-stone logs and drainpipe tunnels covered with climbers.

Climbing trees

The most traditional and in many ways the most exciting garden feature to climb is a tree, which has the added benefit of fitting in easily with the planting scheme. The ideal climbing tree will have spreading branches that swoop down to within easy reach of the ground. Apple trees often develop limbs that turn them into good climbing trees. Trees to avoid are those with brittle branches such as *Robinia pseudoacacia* (false acacia) and any that develop dead wood. Even dead trees, if the wood is sound, can be turned into horizontal climbing features.

If the lower limbs of the tree are out of reach, a rope ladder, knotted rope or purpose-made wooden ladder lashed to the tree can bridge the gap. You can set the height of the lowest rung to exclude younger children. The rope should be synthetic nylon or polypropylene (more durable than hemp), and should have a half-ton breaking strength; usually a 9–10mm (³⁄₈in) diameter man-made rope will provide this.

Large branches or tree trunks left to lie not only look decorative but also make wonderful climbing structures for children.

Fixing a rope to a tree

When you are fixing items such as a rope ladder, swing seat, trapeze bar, trapeze rings, twizzler, monkey swing or a rope to a branch, tie the rope (or ropes) securely to the branch with a bowline knot (fig 1). Next throw the long end or ends over the branch. This is to make sure that the swing does not wear on the knot, but constantly wraps and unwraps itself around the branch (fig 2). Bark can be very abrasive so, before fixing the rope to the tree, check that the contact point is smooth. If you are fixing a plain rope, a large knot on the bottom is good for grip while climbing on and for sitting when swinging; use a double overhand knot for this (fig 3).

Always check at least once every six months, and preferably monthly, that the knots on any ropes are safe, and replace immediately any rope that starts to fray or show signs of wear. Also check regularly that the branch is still able to support the load that it is required to carry (remembering that a child's weight increases yearly), that it is not rotting, and that any ropes used are not constricting the growth of the tree.

Fixing a peg into a dead tree

For climbing, you can set a dead tree trunk upright in concrete (obtain dead tree trunks from parks or sawmills). Check the security of the fixing and soundness of wood at least twice yearly. Have a maximum fall height of 2m (6½ft) and lay a safety surface.

1 Saw off unsafe/badly placed branches (leave longer if they will carry a swing).
2 Ensure the wood shows no decay.
3 Drill holes 100mm (4in) deep to take 25–35mm (1–1⅜in) diameter dowels at suitable intervals for climbing.
4 Saw off 300mm (1ft) lengths of ramin dowel; glue into the holes.
5 Saw 50mm (2in) lengths from a 60mm (2½in) diameter dowel, round edges and glue to each peg to cap.

This adventure maze is designed to encourage a wide range of play activities. All the elements are simple and inexpensive to construct, and they work well together as well as individually. Designed for an area of about 11 x 11m (36 x 36ft), the maze could be adapted to fit a much smaller space.

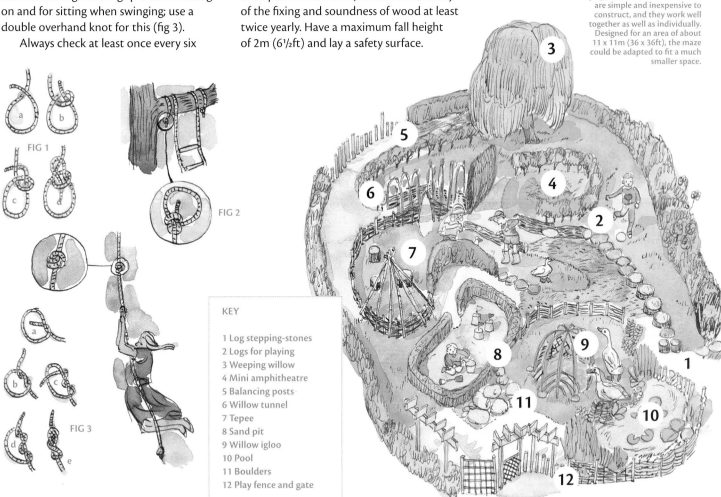

FIG 1

FIG 2

FIG 3

KEY

1 Log stepping-stones
2 Logs for playing
3 Weeping willow
4 Mini amphitheatre
5 Balancing posts
6 Willow tunnel
7 Tepee
8 Sand pit
9 Willow igloo
10 Pool
11 Boulders
12 Play fence and gate

PROJECT: A CLIMBING PERGOLA

This pergola/climbing frame is designed to provide a play structure that can be converted into a conventional pergola, providing a framework for climbing plants, when the children are older. Ensure that the siting of the pergola works in design terms both now and in the future.

The design shown here may be adapted to suit different size gardens. The basic unit is a pergola arch with six uprights. In most situations I favour a pergola formed from a series of archways, with definite gaps between them, as this style is usually more easily absorbed into the garden setting. Another advantage is that different archways can become different play features, perhaps one with a trapeze, another with a scramble net and so on. The highly visible archways could be treated as purely ornamental features and covered with climbers, and the less visible ones used for play. It is also possible to link a number of archways with horizontals to make a much larger structure.

The surface underneath the pergola should be a safety surface such as bark or gravel (see page 47). Rounded particle gravel intermingled with plants may complement the surrounding garden, unless your pergola leads through light woodland in which case bark chippings may be more appropriate.

Climbing plants

Site plants away from the areas used for climbing, as the dead leaves could lead to damp, slippery surfaces. Recommended plants include the thornless, cerise pink *Rosa* 'Zephirine Drouhin', which will thrive even on the north-facing side of the pergola; the white wisteria, *Wisteria venusta;* and

many of the honeysuckles, which provide fragrant, sometimes evergreen, cover. Limit the selection to two or three species to give a strong, unified effect.

Finally, check the pergola at least twice a year to make sure that it is structurally sound, that the wood is in good shape, and that the bolts and fixings are sound.

You will need

For a double arch

- 12 vertical posts (**A**), 100 x 100mm x 2.9m (4 x 4in x 9ft 8in) tanalized softwood, (PAR)
- Four horizontal front beams (**B**), 100 x 100mm x 2.3m (4 x 4in x 7ft 8in) tanalized softwood, (PAR)
- Two horizontal side beams (**C**), 100 x 100mm x 4.5m (4 x 4in x 15ft) tanalized softwood, (PAR)
- 10 ladder rungs (**D**), 38 x 50mm x 1m (1½ x 2 x 40in) tanalized softwood, (PAR), free of knots
- Four ladder rungs (**E**), 38 x 50 x 550mm (1½ x 2 x 22in) tanalized softwood, (PAR), free of knots
- 20 coach bolts with protective coating 220mm (9in) long, M10 (10mm/³⁄₈in) in diameter, with single coil washers, washers and nuts
- Countersunk zinc-plated No. 12 screws,

75mm (3in)
- Concrete, 1.25m³ (1.6 cu.yd) 1:6 mix cement: ballast
- One barrow load of free-draining material
- Gravel to surface
- Non-toxic wood stain

Tools

- Hand saw • Spade • Shovel • Drill
- Countersink bit • Spirit level • Spanner
- Screwdriver • Hacksaw • Fine flat file • Plane
- String lines and pins

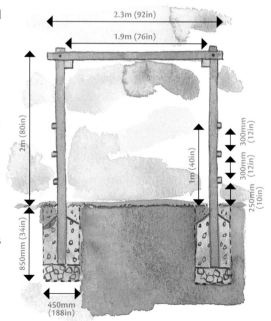

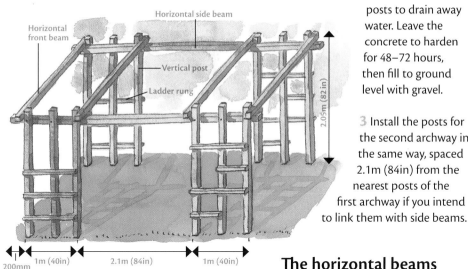

Labels on diagram:
- Horizontal front beam
- Horizontal side beam
- Vertical post
- Ladder rung
- 2.05m (82in)
- 200mm (8in)
- 1m (40in)
- 2.1m (84in)
- 1m (40in)

posts to drain away water. Leave the concrete to harden for 48–72 hours, then fill to ground level with gravel.

3 Install the posts for the second archway in the same way, spaced 2.1m (84in) from the nearest posts of the first archway if you intend to link them with side beams.

The archway

1 Decide where to site the pergola and mark out a rectangle 2.1 x 1m (84 x 40in) with crossed string lines. Four of the posts stand in the corners of the rectangle. The remaining two posts are centred between the corner posts on the short sides, making these three posts at 450mm (18in) centres. Dig out a trench for each set of three posts, 850mm (34in) deep by 1350 x 450mm (54 x 18in), centred on the short sides of the rectangle. Place a 50mm (2in) depth of free-draining material in the base of each trench.

2 Position the posts in the trenches and brace them with scrap wood so that they stay upright. Pour in the concrete to within 200mm (8in) of the top, checking again that the posts are vertical with a spirit level. Angle the surface of the concrete away from the

The horizontal beams

4 Clamp or tie the horizontal side beams (C) to the posts, or ask two helpers to support them in position, while you drill holes through the vertical posts and the beams to take the bolts. Fix each side beam with a bolt, washer, single coil washer and nut at each of its junctions with a vertical post, to link the two archways.

5 Position the horizontal front beams (B) on top of the horizontal side beams as shown. Drill holes to take the bolts and then fix them with a bolt, washer, single coil washer and nut to the vertical post at each end. Next trim off the top of the vertical posts, leaving about 50mm (2in) proud of the horizontal front beams.

6 The ladder rungs are fixed to the vertical posts with two countersunk 75mm (3in) screws at each station. Counterbore the holes so that the screw heads sit 6mm (½in) below the surface. If the tops of the rungs are rounded they are easier for children to grip so, using a plane, create a smooth, gently rounded top on each one. The exact position of the rungs will depend on the particular feature that you are creating, but do not make them closer than 175mm (7in) or they may form a trap.

7 Cut off all protruding bolt threads flush with the nuts using a hacksaw. File the ends smooth and dab with enamel paint. Treat the wood with two coats of preservative wood stain.

Additional features

8 Attach rope ladders, a trapeze, a monkey swing, a scramble net or a climbing rope. Take care to site a swing well away from other play elements in order to prevent accidents. It should be hung from one of the middle horizontal front beams, so that it is anchored in both directions, and fitted with a rubber safety seat.

The single arch unit can be used alone (left), in a sequence of three or more, or joined to a second arch with horizontal beams (centre and right).

PLAYING BALL

Whatever the age, sex and number of your children, it is likely that ball games of one sort or another are popular. If you can incorporate into your garden a flat area of lawn where, for example, badminton, rounders, softball or short tennis can be played, it will pay big dividends. The planting must be tough, established and up to the job. Bearing in mind that the plants may be trampled in the search for a lost ball, use shrubs that will shoot back, such as *Cotoneaster* spp., *Kerria japonica*, *Rhus typhina* and buddleias (see pp. 118–119). Alternatively, limit play to the dormant season when the herbaceous plants are safe below ground.

Certain ball games can be played with no grass. Boules, or petanque, for example, is best on a rougher surface such as gravel, making the game less predictable and limiting the travel of the ball. Palas can be played on any surface and in very small spaces; you need only a wooden bat (similar to a table tennis bat) and a ball. There is no net, no court, and no rules. The aim is to keep the rallies going as long as possible, and the closer you stand the faster the play. A basketball net can be fixed in many places, and keeps children of a wide age range amused.

Tennis is highly popular, but few people have the space for the real thing. Short tennis, a scaled-down version using softer balls and lighter rackets, can be played in the average garden (see below).

If your plants are more important than sport, balls on elastic for the children are the answer. You can obtain a baseball batting trainer set, a swing ball and circles tennis, none of which require a large area to play in.

Short tennis

Short tennis is an excellent garden game for all ages. The strokes and rules are similar to lawn tennis, but the rackets are smaller and lighter, the ball is softer and the court a lot smaller. The court size for short tennis is 13.4 x 6.1m (44 x 20ft) with a centre line for serving; there should be a minimum of 1.8m (6ft) space at either end of the court and 1.5m (5ft) at the sides. The net is 790mm (2ft 7in) high at the centre and 830mm (2ft 9in) at the posts.

Clock golf

Clock golf can be played on any fairly level lawn. Design the clock face as large as required, make a hole in the centre, mark out the 12 numbers of the clock and put a flag and cup in the hole. The object is to pot the ball from each number. All you need is one ball and one club; the number and age of the players is limitless. If you feel

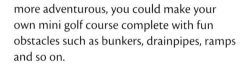

more adventurous, you could make your own mini golf course complete with fun obstacles such as bunkers, drainpipes, ramps and so on.

Badminton

This is ideally suited to the garden lawn. Two or four players can play at one time. The court measures 13.4 x 6.1m (44 x 20ft) and the net is 760mm (2ft 6in) deep; the top edge is 1520mm (5ft) from the ground in the centre and 1550mm

(5ft 1in) at the posts. The rackets and shuttlecocks are relatively inexpensive, as are the posts and nets. The court needs careful siting as wind can disrupt play.

Deck tennis/quoits

As the name suggests, this game was designed to be played on board ship and so is ideal for a small garden. A net 1420mm (4ft 8in) high is strung centrally across a rectangular court measuring 4.3 x 8.2m

(14 x 27ft). A 'neutral zone' that extends 450mm (18in) into the court on either side of the net is marked out. The game requires 2–4 players and a quoit (a small round rubber ring) that is thrown single-handedly across the net, caught single-handedly and then instantly returned from the same position. Points are won when your opponents fail to return the quoit into the court, and lost if it touches the ground in the neutral zone. When you reach 15 points you have won the set, and three or five sets are usual.

French cricket

This simple, popular game can be enjoyed from three years old upwards. A cricket bat, baseball bat, or tennis racquet is used to shield the batsman's lower legs, while the other players try to get him out by hitting him below the knee with the ball. It is usually played with a tennis ball, as anything harder could be lethal. The rules vary, but are commonly that the batsman is out if a fieldsman catches the ball with both hands, or single-handedly with one bounce. The batsman clocks up runs by passing the bat around his legs in circles.

Soccer

This is among the most popular ball games, particularly for boys. Assuming you have some lawn, a goal carefully sited to minimize the impact on plants may well be very popular. If your garden is large enough, you could designate a specific patch and ensure that the planting around this area is sturdy.

Here a rustic soccer goal has been designed to fit into some low box hedging, which protects the rough plants behind.

The ideal surface for boules is gravel. Shown here is a bound golden gravel, though the larger-particle loose gravel used for driveways would work.

SAND AND WATER

If you have ever watched the absorbed concentration with which children play with sand and water, you will not have the slightest doubt that they are, in some way, satisfying a basic need. Although public parks often provide sand pits and paddling pools for children, the attraction of having your own smaller version for everyday use is immense. Small children derive great pleasure from sand and it forms a safe play area, but even older children will become engrossed in creating sand villages complete with turrets, moats and bridges, often entertaining younger children into the bargain.

Siting a sand pit

Sand is inexpensive, readily available and, providing the edge treatment of the sand pit fits in well with the surroundings (see p. 59), it will look attractive in most gardens. Even in the smallest garden, an area of sand in which several children can play together is a good investment. While the children are very small, position the sand pit fairly close to the house, where it can be easily observed, but keep it away from doorways as sand has a habit of travelling. If you site the sand pit in a sunny spot, you may need to provide umbrella shade in high summer. The shade of a tree may be suitable if you are prepared to remove fallen leaves from the sand.

When you are designing and siting your sand pit, do not necessarily think of it in isolation, but consider combining it with other play features. For instance, you could make a large, sunken sand pit, contained with log edging, and grow a willow teepee beside it. Alternatively, a low seat and table made from simple log rounds form an ideal 'work station' for hours of play.

If you don't have the space to build a larger sand pit, simple solutions are containers, such as a tractor tyre (lined with a geotextile membrane), or a large, ornamental bowl or trough. You can buy ready-made, raised timber sand pits that blend into the garden more readily than the brightly coloured plastic versions. A timber sand pit is easy to make at home, with planks forming the four sides and diagonal seats across the corners.

If you are siting the sand pit directly by the house, a more formal solution, such as a sunken pit designed as part of the terrace using coordinated materials, may be the answer. Partially surround the pit with raised walls, which could be wood, stone or brick, and about 300–400mm (1–1ft 4in) high to form additional seating and help to contain the sand that enthusiastic users inevitably hurl about with gay abandon. Leave a break in the wall so that any travelling sand can be easily swept back in. When the children have outgrown the sand pit, the sunken area can be filled in with plants, paved or made into a small water feature.

This water channel made from granite setts has a water supply and can be drained.

Water play

Sand and water complement one another for children's play. If you do not want to site a pool of water by the sand pit, a large refillable bowl or trough would contribute enormously to the play value of the sand. Add some pebbles and boulders that can form dams, walls and bridges.

Paddling pools are the traditional way of providing water play in the garden and, if you are looking for an alternative to the ready-made plastic variety, a more permanent and attractive form to make is illustrated on pp. 60–61. However, water for play can be incorporated into the scheme in many other ways.

An old-fashioned hand pump that gushes on to an area of slightly dished paving forms a delightful play feature. Alternatively, make a small, dished pool out of concrete to hold pebbles, shells and sparkling clean water. The pool could be filled with a hose and drained through a plug hole. An adjoining stretch of pebbles, shingle and sand would provide complementary additions for play.

Even simpler options include a large bowl, old sink or waterproofed wooden barrel cut in half. Any of these, positioned under a tap and surrounded with boulders and shingle, will provide excellent play value.

This drainable paddling pool combined with a wooden-edged sand pit is set flush with the ground.

Carved from local weathered stone, this small sand pit is ideal for young children.

BUILDING A SAND PIT

If you decide to make your own sand pit, a good size is about 1.2m (4ft) square, with the minimum size for small children to play in about 700mm (2ft 4in) square. If you choose to build it with raised edges, these should be approximately 380mm (15in) high, so that smaller children can clamber over them. The same measurements apply for the depth of the pit, if you decide to make a sunken one, but only fill a sunken sand pit to a depth of about 220mm (9in) to avoid losing too much sand over the edges.

Laying the base

When you make the sand pit, whether it is raised or sunken, it must have a free-draining base, so that the sand has a chance to dry out. If it is permanently wet, bacteria, algae and similar undesirables will breed in it and turn it sour. One method for adequate drainage is to lay old paving slabs over the base with 10mm (⅓in) gaps between them. If you are on extremely free-draining soil, it is possible just to place a layer of geotextile membrane over the base of the pit, and put the sand directly on top of this.

If your soil is not well drained, put in a 50–100mm (2–4in) deep layer of free-draining hardcore or gravel over the base, laid to a fall. Blind the hardcore if necessary with some sand to form a smoothish top, then lay the geotextile membrane with the sand on top.

Filling the sand pit

Use the sand sold especially for sand pits. Play sand is a light-coloured sand, which means it does not stain clothes, it is lime-free, and has been washed and graded. Building sand is not suitable, as it stains clothes and, when wet, can form a yellow sludge not good for high-quality sand castles.

Having filled your sand pit, you should provide a cover to prevent the local fauna using it for their less attractive purposes. The design of the cover should not be solid, as exposure to air and sunlight keeps the sand sweet. An attractive and relatively easy-to-make cover that children can remove themselves can be formed from strips of wood laid side by side with gaps in between, linked by two or more webbing bands stapled along the top. Alternatively, stretch bird or chicken netting over the top of the sand pit.

Instead of trying to hide or disguise a sand pit, this delightful boat design illustrates how to turn it into a garden feature.

Sand pit edging designs

For all five designs the sand is laid over a geotextile membrane that, in turn, is laid over a 50–100mm (2–4in) depth of free-draining, blinded hardcore or coarse gravel.

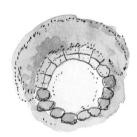

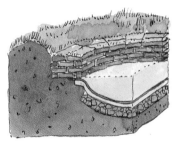

GRASS BENCH This grass bench surround has been made from turves. Cut turves about 50–100mm (2–4in) thick and lay the first layer on to the soil platform, building up the bench in layers until it is 100mm (4in) below the lawn surface. This should be carried out in the autumn or spring, and the turves should be well watered until the top turves become established. The grass will form a vertical green wall fairly quickly. Trim with shears to keep it short. Reinforce some of the walls with tougher material such as logs.

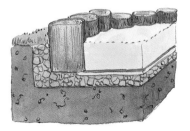

A CIRCLE OF LOGS This surround is made from a ring of sawn logs that are set into the ground. A suitable log ranges in size from about 200mm (8in) to 300mm (12in) in diameter. Set the logs into a trench about 300mm (12in) deep, butting them closely together. Ram earth back into the trench to secure the logs.

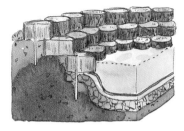

MINI AMPHITHEATRE If you have an existing, shallow dell in your garden you could construct this mini amphitheatre from stepped logs. The logs are about 300mm (1ft) long by a similar width. The bottom level of logs is set into the base of the slope on the free-draining surface, fixed with a metal reinforcing bar through each log (drill the log first) and driven into the ground to a depth of about 500mm (20in). The middle level is set into the slope, with the logs joined together with metal staples or skew nailing. The top layer is also fixed with metal bars driven into the ground. Check that the structure is safe and secure.

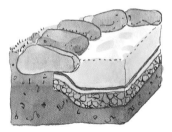

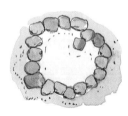

BOULDERS Ideal for sitting on, smoothly rounded boulders form an interesting, irregular edge with crevices for play. Leave a mowing margin of about 150mm (6in) wide, filling it with a suitable material such as cockle shells. If natural boulders cannot be found, make substitutes out of concrete. Dig a boulder-shaped hole and line with polythene. Pour concrete into a soil mould and leave to harden (48–72 hours).

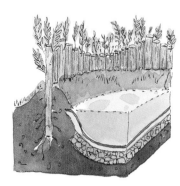

WILLOWS Here a living screen fence of willows has been set on a mounded bank to provide a secluded sand-pit-cum-den with a beach dune feel. To make this feature, form a gentle mound around the proposed sand pit using the soil that was excavated. Take slim branches about 20mm (³⁄₄in) in diameter from a vigorous willow, such as *Salix alba*, during the dormant season, and push them into the soil mound to a depth of 300mm (12in), leaving variable heights exposed to create a pleasing irregular edge. Water well regularly, weave in new growths to fill out the walls and trim them to the required height.

KEY

 Top layer of sand

 Geotextile membrane

 Free-draining hardcore 50–100mm (2–4in) deep

PROJECT: A PADDLING POOL

This small paddling pool, which is constructed using a heavy-gauge butyl liner and is flush with the ground, is filled from the hosepipe and has a drain allowing it to be emptied and cleaned periodically. The size of 1.5 x 1.5m (5 x 5ft) by 450mm (18in) deep can be varied according to your needs. Whatever the depth, make sure that the children are watched while the pool is in use, as it is possible to drown in less than 150mm (6in) of water. Butyl does puncture, so treat it with respect. When the pool is not being used, put a protective safety cover over it, anchored in position, rather than leaving it empty and vulnerable to falling debris, curious animals and the like.

You will need

- Heavy-duty butyl liner, 3.5 x 3.5m (11ft 6in x 11ft 6in) for the size of the pool shown here; available in black, blue or stone colour (the stone colour is recommended)
- Underlay, of the same area as above
- Weak mortar, 1:1:8 mix (cement:lime: building sand), 0.3m³ (0.4 cu.yd) for lining pool
- Free-draining gravel or hardcore, 0.6m³ (0.8 cu.yd)
- uPVC threaded tank connector, 50mm (2in) (see Suppliers, page 128)
- Universal plug, 100mm (4in) in diameter, to cover tank connector
- uPVC waste pipe, 50mm (2in) in diameter; length depends on position of soakaway
- uPVC 90° elbow, 50mm (2in)
- uPVC stop valve, 50mm (2in)
- uPVC soil pipe, 1m (39in) by 100mm (4in) in diameter
- Access cover for soil pipe
- Concrete, 1:6 mix (cement:ballast), 0.4m³ (0.5 cu.yd)
- Mortar, 1:5 mix (cement:building sand) for paving

- Mastic sealant
- Solvent cement for uPVC
- 12 paving slabs, 450 x 450mm (18 x 18in)
- 4 paving slabs, 450 x 600mm (18 x 24in)

Tools
- Spade • Shovel • Pick axe • Club hammer
- Steel float • Spirit level • Stanley knife
- Scissors • Hacksaw • Half-round file
- Large spanner

Digging out the pool

1 First dig out the pool itself to 150mm (6in) below the required final level of the base. Make the sides of the pool about 10° off the vertical – 100mm (4in) further in at the base in a 600mm (24in) deep excavation.

2 From the centre of the base, dig a trench for the drainage pipe 150mm (6in) wide by 100mm (4in) deep to the edge of the pool base, then continue through the sidewall to the position of the proposed soakaway or drain. The fall can be minimal, as the weight of water alone will drain the pool. To make a soakaway, dig out a small area at the end of the trench about 600mm (24in) square to a depth of 900mm (36in) below ground level.

3 Attach a 90° elbow to the bottom of the tank connector and run a 50mm (2in) uPVC pipe from the elbow to the stop valve. Connect a second length from the valve to the soakaway, to finish 300mm (12in) into the soakaway. Lay the assembled pipework in the trench, and prop the tank connector in position vertically so that the top is flush with the final base level of the pool.

4 To allow access to the stop valve, cut a length of 100mm (4in) diameter uPVC soil pipe to fit over and around the valve. Cut a notch in the bottom so that the pipe straddles the drainage pipe and sits on the bottom of the trench. Place a suitable cover over the top. This should be just below ground level, to prevent feet getting caught in it.

5 Prop a board over the end of the trench at the soakaway to contain the soil, then

back-fill the trench, compacting the soil firmly to the contour of the disturbed side wall. Level off the soil inside the pool flush with the excavated base. Fill the soakaway with free-draining hardcore to within 200mm (8in) of ground level, then top up with soil to ground level.

Preparing the base and surround

6 Cover the tank connector, to keep out debris, then excavate foundations for the slabs to a depth of 225mm (9in) below their base. Lay 100mm (4in) of well-compacted gravel or hardcore over the entire base of the pool, leaving 50mm (2in) of the tank connector exposed.

7 Cut a 50mm (2in) length of the soil pipe and fit it centrally around the connector, to act as shuttering, then lay a 300mm (12in) diameter circle of 1:6 mix concrete, 50mm (2in) thick, around the protruding connector. Level the concrete with the top of the tank connector.

8 Lay a firm base of hardcore 100mm (4in) thick over the ledges for the slabs, followed by a 100mm (4in) bed of 1:6 mix concrete; prop 100mm (4in) boards above the hardcore,

angled to the slope of the walls, to contain the concrete. Check concrete is level then leave to set for 48–72 hours.

9 Cover the base of the pool all around the concrete surround to the tank connector with a 50mm (2in) thick layer of weak mortar mix and trowel the same mix up the walls.

Fitting the liner

10 Remove the top nut and washer of the tank connector. Next fit the underlay, covering the base and sides of the pool and the paving slab foundations. Cut a small hole around the top of the tank connector and tuck in the underlay around it. Lay the liner over the underlay, working from one side. At the centre of the base, cut a hole just smaller than the tank connector. Apply mastic

sealant to the bottom nut and washer, and to the underside of the liner at this point, then stretch the liner gently over the top of the tank connector and on to the washer. Apply more mastic to the top of the liner and to the top washer and nut, position the washer, then screw on the nut tightly to seal the liner to the tank connector.

11 Lay the liner over the rest of the pool, gathering it neatly into definite folds rather than leaving lots of small creases. Find a suitable plug, such as a large universal sink plug, to sit inside the top of the tank connector and cover the outer pipe (it need not make a watertight seal).

12 Lay the paving slabs over the liner on a continuous bed of 1:5 mix mortar, 25mm (1in) thick. They should overhang the pool by 20mm (3/4in), and be horizontal and completely level with each other. When the mortar has set (48–72 hours), the pool can be filled.

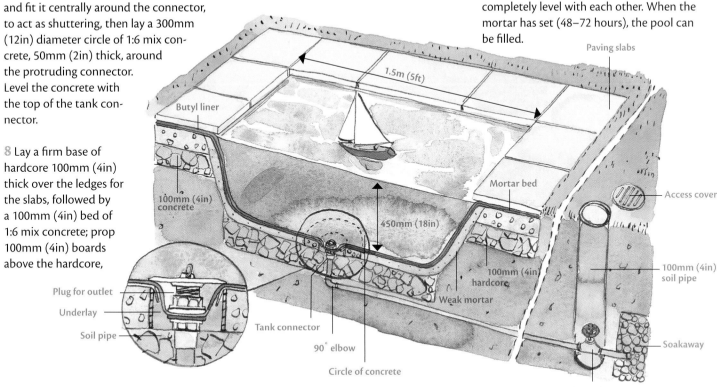

Butyl liner

1.5m (5ft)

450mm (18in)

Paving slabs

Mortar bed

Access cover

100mm (4in) concrete

100mm (4in) soil pipe

100mm (4in) hardcore

Weak mortar

Plug for outlet

Underlay

Soil pipe

Tank connector

90° elbow

Circle of concrete

Soakaway

Stop valve

OUTDOOR LIVING

A well-planned garden should be at the hub of family life, providing an attractive setting for a host of memorable occasions including birthday teas, picnics, informal barbecues and summer siestas. On top of all this, it can also fulfil the oldest role of a garden as a supplier of food for the family. Today there are countless vegetable varieties to maximize yield and flavour, while many are attractive enough to add visual appeal as well.

EATING AND ENTERTAINING

Eating outdoors is an almost unbeatable pleasure in a warm and sheltered spot, surrounded by luxuriant foliage and a colourful haze of blossom, with a little dappled shade throwing a pattern across your plate. The informality of these outdoor events makes them particularly suitable for entertaining guests of all ages. Accidental spillages matter much less, children can come and go and, in the case of barbecues, everyone helps with the cooking.

However, eating outdoors can also be utterly unenjoyable if the environment is not right. We have all experienced problems of one kind or another, whether it be gusts of wind blowing food off the table, or sizzling in the sun on a sea of red-hot paving with wasps driving you crazy.

The perfect site

The main attributes for a good outdoor eating area are shelter from the wind and a warm, sunny spot. Often the most convenient place to eat in the garden is directly outside French windows leading to a kitchen; this has obvious advantages for ferrying food to and fro.

However, directly outside the kitchen may not be the best place for an eating area. For example, there may be a more sheltered site further into the garden where there are no eddying gusts. Perhaps being deeper in the garden this site will also be more lush and tranquil and provide some privacy. Another option is to designate a small area for everyday eating and a larger area for entertaining a number of guests. These outdoor eating areas tend to become the hub of the garden, providing a focal point for family life in much the same way that a large kitchen does in a house, so it will rarely be a wasted allocation of space.

Improving the site

If wind or sun is a problem and you cannot move your eating area, bear in mind that you can alter the microclimate dramatically in a short space of time. For example, our everyday eating area is small – just 4m (11ft) square and is on the north side of the house, on top of a hill, and therefore exposed to unceasing south-westerly winds. More often than not in the summer, the family spills out for breakfast, elevenses, lunch, tea and supper. Despite its unpropitious aspect and elevation, the area has been made even more comfortable by planting a series of windbreaks, including hedges, trees, a willow hurdle fence and some large mallows.

It is also possible to design a single eating area to accommodate larger numbers. Extra seating can be provided by wide, shallow steps, perhaps with removable cushions. Walls of a suitable height are also invaluable to seat extra guests, whether they form the edge of a raised bed or are free-standing.

A dining room outdoors

It can be very successful to design your eating area as an outdoor dining room, partly enclosed by walls, a trellis, hedging, shrubs or masonry. Consider adding a partial roof for shade. This could be a light, overhead timber structure, a trellis adorned with climbers, a boldly striped awning fixed to the house or just a simple umbrella. Furnish the 'room' with bold collections of pots to add interest, colour and focal points allowing the table and chairs to provide the main focus.

If the convenience factor of having a permanent barbecue appeals to you, and you decide to include it in the area, do make sure that it enhances the area and does not dominate it (see page 70). The sight and sound of water adds another dimension to the eating area, and it may well make sense to position a water feature where it will be appreciated frequently. It is also then ideally sited to cool the wine!

If the eating area is to be used as an outdoor room, it is necessary to provide lighting so that it can be used in the evening. General illumination can be achieved by siting a lamp high up on an adjacent wall; this will allow you to move around safely and see what you are eating. More atmospheric effects result from spotlighting particular features or plants; the lights are generally sited low down so that they shine up at the chosen feature.

This orchard eating area is very simple and delightfully shaded and leafy. It belongs to a large family whose numbers frequently swell with visiting friends. A sheltered glade is provided by fruit trees, creating an effect that is charmingly informal, lush and green.

This small trellis pavilion was designed and built by Peter Farrell for his own garden. It not only encloses a small formal eating area but also frames a pleasant view down to his orchard.

A large white parasol completely transforms this eating area, giving it a luxurious colonial feel. Moveable shade is very practical when eating outside as it can be set up to take advantage of cooling breezes and minimize cold draughts.

How much easier and enjoyable life becomes when children can entertain their friends outside! This simple log table with chairs is easy to make, ideal for a small garden and makes an attractive addition to any informal garden corner.

65

DESIGN OF THE TERRACE

The terrace or main paved area in a garden is, more often than not, next to the house. It is a bridge between the house and garden and often acts as a visual tie linking the two spaces.

When you start to design a terrace area, the priority is to decide what character it should have and, in order to create a visual link, it makes sense that the style, scale and materials for the terrace complement the character of the house.

Design considerations

The size of the house governs the size of the terrace area. A tall, imposing house makes a small area of paving look a little ridiculous so, in this instance, it pays to make the paved area proportionally wide as well as long. To avoid creating a wasteland of paving on a large terrace, the area could be divided with patterns in the paving. A pattern might, for example, be laid in line with door and/or window openings.

If you have a small house or cottage, a proportionally small terrace is perfectly in keeping. However, if you have a tiny house, a very generous paved area is extremely useful and, so long as the large area of paving is broken up into smaller areas with a pattern, it can still look in harmony with the house.

When deciding on the size of the terrace, do not be too restrained. An attractive, functional family garden needs a good-sized paved area. It will probably be highly visible all year round, and usable for at least six months of the year. Work out the area required for the garden furniture and leave generous amounts of clearance around access points. Then decide where you are going to position borders and plants. Almost

invariably the junction between the house and the paving looks better as a broad border that will soften the edge of the house and help bind it to the garden.

There are some basic design principles to consider:
• do not skimp on the size but make a good, usable space
• avoid large, unbroken areas of paving by introducing a pattern
• relate the scale and positioning of architectural details of the house in the paving patterns
• avoid a run of paving going up to the house
• plant generous borders between the house and terrace to link house and garden.

Paving ideas

Paving is one of the most costly features of a garden, but cheaper forms of cover, such as bound or loose gravel, may be combined with more expensive hard materials. Areas of planting can also be incorporated to form patterns. An attractive chequer-board effect terrace can be created by alternating squares of paving with squares of *Sagina glabra*. In the most used areas, such as those with chairs and tables, a covering of paving alone is more convenient.

Another idea is to combine paved areas with small squares of grass to form regular patterns. The patterns can look stunning and the grassy areas soften the overall effect. Alternatively, lay paving with 20mm (³⁄₄in) joints leaving out whole slabs in places and planting and/or gravelling the joints and gaps with one or more varieties of very low-growing plants – *Thymus serpyllum* 'Snowdrift', for example.

This terrace has been sited in a convenient, sheltered spot adjacent to the house. It is further enclosed by high stone walls, creating an enticing and highly usable tiny courtyard.

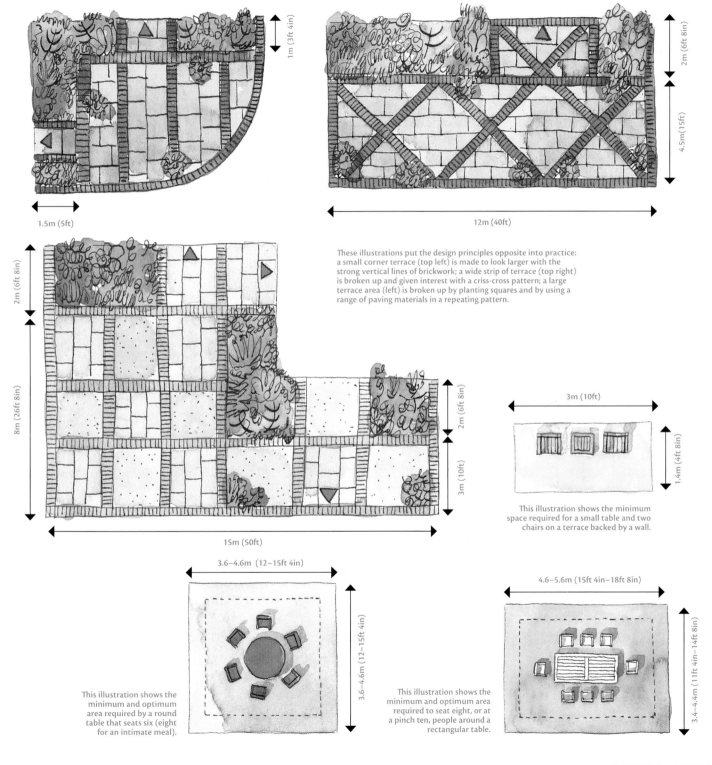

1m (3ft 4in)

2m (6ft 8in)

4.5m (15ft)

1.5m (5ft)

12m (40ft)

2m (6ft 8in)

8m (26ft 8in)

2m (6ft 8in)

3m (10ft)

15m (50ft)

These illustrations put the design principles opposite into practice: a small corner terrace (top left) is made to look larger with the strong vertical lines of brickwork; a wide strip of terrace (top right) is broken up and given interest with a criss-cross pattern; a large terrace area (left) is broken up by planting squares and by using a range of paving materials in a repeating pattern.

3m (10ft)

1.4m (4ft 8in)

This illustration shows the minimum space required for a small table and two chairs on a terrace backed by a wall.

3.6–4.6m (12–15ft 4in)

3.6–4.6m (12–15ft 4in)

This illustration shows the minimum and optimum area required by a round table that seats six (eight for an intimate meal).

4.6–5.6m (15ft 4in–18ft 8in)

3.4–4.4m (11ft 4in–14ft 8in)

This illustration shows the minimum and optimum area required to seat eight, or at a pinch ten, people around a rectangular table.

A Low-Maintenance Design

If you have a terrace or a paved back garden, there are many design elements, from paving materials to container planting, that can enhance the outside space.

Paving

When selecting materials, perhaps the most important consideration is that the paved areas near the house complement the house materials to give a sense of harmony.

Gravel The least expensive hard ground cover. Edge the gravelled area with a generous band of paving slabs, brick or granite setts to prevent the gravel being taken indoors on shoes.

Bound gravel Made of very small particles that, when watered and rolled, compact into a firm surface, which is less likely to be carried into the house and is also suitable for wheelchairs.

Wood Options include diagonally laid decking or hardwood log rounds placed vertically to give a network of uniform or variably sized circles. Fill the gaps with a green carpeter such as the splendid *Soleirolia soleirolii* (babies' tears) and/or bark mulch for a woodland feel.

Stone slabs Can be an expensive choice, although there are excellent reproduction stone paving slabs available. Real stone slabs evoke a traditional feel and complement many other materials.

Granite setts Small-unit paving materials are ideal for making a small area look bigger. Setts are a wonderful way of introducing patterns, such as bands or curves.

Bricks Usually laid in herringbone, basket weave or stretcher bond. All bricks must be of a suitable quality for paving, otherwise they will shatter in heavy frosts.

Pebbles Pebble paving and mosaics have a special charm with their colour variation, allowing both abstract and figurative patterns to be made. Also useful as a deterrent paving, to stop people cutting corners and walking too close to planting.

Roof tiles Laid on edge in blocks, circles or bands, the small unit size of a roof tile makes it suitable for a wide range of patterned effects.

Terracotta tiles With their rustic charm and warm pink colour, terracotta tiles can make a paved area look very much like an outside room.

Steps

Steps provide an interesting link between house and terrace, or terrace and garden, and should be exploited to the full. They may be wide and grand, with deep treads and shallow risers, climbing the slope gently, or they may be very steep, narrow and winding, arousing curiosity. When organizing the levels of a terrace, avoid a single step, as it tends to become a hazard. Basic steps can be transformed by lining the edges with potted plants, especially scented varieties.

These steps display a wonderful assortment of abundantly planted pots that make them appear much more dramatic than if they were unadorned.

Containers

The clever use of containers adds another dimension to any part of the paved area, bringing many possibilities by increasing the range of plants you can grow in the garden. Plants such as citrus fruits can be moved outdoors in the warmer months and brought in to a kinder climate in the cold periods. They allow you to create soil conditions that you may not have in the garden and are a useful source of mobile colour, allowing you to introduce spots of intense colour created by flowers at their peak.

Children appreciate the small scale of planting that a container provides, and they should be encouraged to create their own small container planting. A 400mm (16in) high pot is at a convenient height for a young child and large enough to provide some scope for planting. My six-year-old planted one with leeks and a red cabbage that did far better than those in the vegetable garden.

Plant maintenance

The drawback with plants in containers is the amount of time it takes to keep them in good condition throughout the summer. If you are an infrequent family gardener, make sure that you insert a semi-automatic watering system inside the pots before the hot weather begins. They are available through specialist suppliers (see page 128).

Alternatively, limit the pot inhabitants to those plants that flourish in minimal moisture situations, such as box, yucca, agaves and the chusan palm. Add a few groups of bulbs, such as tulips, that thrive on a good baking and the scene will be both attractive and undemanding.

Most proprietary composts should contain sufficient nutrients for healthy growth. However, at the height of the growing season it may be necessary to supplement this once a week with some liquid fertilizer.

This exquisite cactus collection belongs to a young plantaholic. Cacti appeal to children with their range of fantastic forms and their occasional stunning blooms.

Gravel is one of the most versatile materials ideally suited to the fluidity of informal settings.

These small paving units are extremely flexible: they can be used to form curves and informal meanders as well as geometric shapes.

A combination of bricks laid flat, pebbles and stone slabs create an intricate pattern. Pebbles are useful for filling odd-shaped gaps.

BARBECUES

Whether you want to knock up an impromptu snack for the family or cook for a party, a barbecue can be a simple, no-fuss way to produce delicious food. The fresh air, the delicious aromas and the easy-going atmosphere that invariably pervade the occasion guarantee that a good time will be had by all generations.

There is no doubt that if you have a permanent structure to cook on outside you will use it more frequently than one that has to be set up for the occasion, and a built-in barbecue can sometimes even enhance a garden. If you do decide to build one, choose a site that is convenient for the transportation of food and blend the barbecue into the surroundings with planting and pots so that it does not dominate the area.

Permanent barbecue

Some of the most effective barbecues are in a recess in the house wall, but obviously this is only feasible in new buildings where they can be planned in. As with any feature, ensure your barbecue fits in with its surroundings. If it is beside the building, use the same material, be it brick, stone or render, and keep the detailing in tune with that around it. Bear in mind that if you burn wood you will get more soot staining the wall. Also, use suitable bricks for the fire bed as some may explode when exposed to intense heat.

My barbecue is an old stone trough that sits on two stone piers against the wall of the house, also stone. I put a layer of thin fire bricks on the base of the sink, as stone can crack or split under intense heat. A shelf at the back keeps any smoke off the wall, but when using charcoal, as we do, this is not usually a problem.

This barbecue, built from reclaimed bricks to match the existing wall, has useful flat surfaces on either side for food preparation and spacious areas beneath for stacking items. The bricks used for the fire bed must be of a suitable quality, as some will explode when exposed to intense heat.

A good way to make a compact heat source is to light the fire in an old galvanized bucket with the bottom knocked out and then gently remove the bucket when the fire gets going.

If you wish to build a stone sink barbecue against a cavity-insulated wall, it is advisable to support the grill tray by a different system, such as bricks on either side, as heat transference through the wall via the metal bars could be a fire hazard. Against a brick wall, use matching brick piers.

Temporary barbecues

Children are always fascinated by fires, and making a well-supervised temporary barbecue will bring them a good deal of pleasure; a few bricks or any suitable materials to hand will suffice. If they can cook food they have provided for themselves, such as sweetcorn they have picked from the vegetable patch, it will add to the illusion of a camping trip.

How to make a stone sink barbecue

The construction of the barbecue is straightforward, though you will probably need to commission a blacksmith to produce the grill tray and the threaded metal sockets in the wall that take the metal bars.

My old stone trough barbecue is used for cooking, and at other times it forms an attractive raised surface useful for sowing or potting.

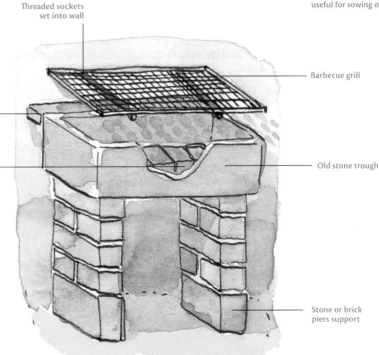

Threaded sockets set into wall

Barbecue grill

Shelf of cut slabs to set barbecue away from wall

Old stone trough

Fire bricks laid on base for protection

Stone or brick piers support

PROJECT: A BARBECUE

The barbecue can be free-standing, or it can be built against an existing wall so that the integrated back wall can be omitted. However, if you are considering building it against an existing wall, bear in mind that the wall will become stained with soot.

If the barbecue is to be built against an existing wall, the bricks should ideally match those already used. Ensure that the new brickwork courses line up with the existing brickwork and tie the barbecue walls to the back wall by screwing angle ties to it every other course above ground. Some bricks explode when exposed to intense heat, so avoid making the fire too close to the edges of the barbecue. It is important not to make the fire directly on the concrete slab as concrete can spit or even explode when heated to high temperatures. For this reason, the brazier tray is housed almost three courses above the slab.

You will need . . . .

- Bricks, special quality, frost-resistant 305 – allow an extra 20 for breakages
- Bricks for the foundations, 108 – allow an extra 10 for breakages
- Paving slabs, 38mm (1½in) thick: two 600 x 900mm (24 x 36in); one 600 x 600mm (24 x 24in)
- Mortar, 1:4 (cement:soft sand) for foundation, and 1:1:6 (cement:lime:soft sand) above ground
- Concrete, 1:6 (cement:all-in ballast) mix for

foundations, approx. ¼m³ (9 cu.ft)
- 15 galvanized angle ties (to tie into existing wall)
- Six metal lugs to take trays (headless coach bolts would suit)
- Mild steel brazier tray, 16 gauge drilled, approximately 600 x 900mm (24 x 36in) with raised lip all around, but take exact measurements when built
- Grill tray, welded mesh, 3mm (⅛in) thick, with steel frame welded round edge and braced in middle

Tools

- Bricklayer's trowel • Brick chisel or bolster
- Club hammer • Pointing trowel • Shovel
- Builder's square • Spirit level • String line

Building the foundation

1 Using a builder's square, mark out on the ground where the walls are to be built. First mark where the centre of the walls will be and then expand these lines outwards by 260mm (10½in) on either side for the 21.5mm (8½in) thick brickwork, and 150mm (6in) on either side for the 102mm (4in) thick brickwork of the back wall. Dig this

area to a depth of 450mm (18in). Work carefully and keep the sides of the trench neat and vertical.

2 Shovel in 150mm (6in) of a 1:6 concrete mix (cement:ballast), then level. Once the concrete has set (allow 48 hours), lay four courses of bricks below ground using a 1:4 (cement:soft sand) mortar.

Laying the brickwork

3 Lay the brickwork using a string line to ensure straightness, and a spirit level to ensure that the bricks are perfectly horizontal and vertical. The mortar mix above ground is 1:1:6 (cement:lime:soft sand). The 215mm (8½in) thick side and centre walls are five courses high, and built using English bond. This consists of alternate courses of headers (bricks laid across the wall thickness) and stretchers (bricks laid lengthways). You will need to cut bricks at both ends of each course to maintain the bond pattern and to bond in the back wall (see illustration).

4 The back wall is 102mm (4in) thick and built using stretcher or running bond (bricks laid lengthways and overlapping half a brick

length in alternate courses). The side walls are built to accommodate the two paving slab sizes used in the design, so check your brickwork against your paving slabs as you progress, bearing in mind that some reproduction stone slabs have irregular sides.

5 The sixth course on the side and centre walls changes to 102mm (4in) thick, leaving a ledge to support the two slabs. It is built in stretcher bond, and is again bonded into the back wall. The coping on one side wall and the rear walls is a half brick on edge.

6 When the mortar has set, lay one 600 x 900mm (24 x 36in) paving slab and the 600 x 600mm (24 x 24in) slab on top of the 215mm (8½in) thick side and centre walls as shown, bedding them on a 1:4 mortar bed. Make sure that the slabs are very securely positioned, with a small gap of about 10mm (³⁄₈in) between them and the back wall.

7 Next, lay the second 600 x 900mm (24 x 36in) paving slab on top of the two 102mm (4in) thick walls without a coping. Finally, back-fill the foundation trenches with soil up to ground level.

Fitting the trays

8 When the brickwork has dried out, it can be drilled and fitted with metal lugs in the ninth, tenth and eleventh courses above ground level to take the brazier tray and grill tray. Measure the exact opening once the walls are built, to ensure a good fit.

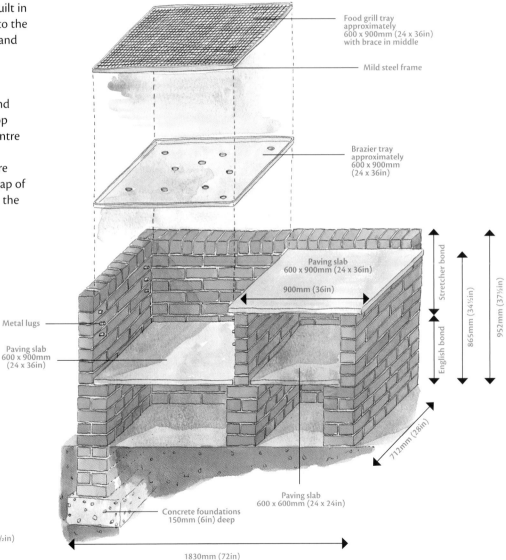

Food grill tray approximately 600 x 900mm (24 x 36in) with brace in middle

Mild steel frame

Brazier tray approximately 600 x 900mm (24 x 36in)

Paving slab 600 x 900mm (24 x 36in)

900mm (36in)

Stretcher bond

865mm (34½in)

952mm (37½in)

Metal lugs

Paving slab 600 x 900mm (24 x 36in)

English bond

712mm (28in)

Paving slab 600 x 600mm (24 x 24in)

Concrete foundations 150mm (6in) deep

1830mm (72in)

Course 7, 9, 11

A

C

Course 6, 8, 10

A

Course 2, 4 and foundation course 2, 4

Back wall

A

A B

Right-hand side wall

Course 1, 3, 5 and foundation course 1, 3

A

Cut brick sizes:
A: ²⁄₃ brick length (150 x 102 x 65mm/ 6 x 4 x 2½in)
B: ½ length + ⅓ width (102 x 30 x 65mm/4 x 1¼ x 2½in)
C: ½ brick length (102 x 102 x 65mm/4 x 4 x 2½in)

FOOD FOR THE FAMILY

As fewer and fewer people have the space or the time to devote large areas of the garden purely to vegetables and fruit, it is becoming increasingly popular to grow certain edible plants laid out in an ornamental fashion.

You may not want to concentrate on vegetables but just pop a few that are attractive and easy to grow into gaps in your flower borders. Some of the faster-growing types can be treated rather like summer bedding, being sown or planted in a mixed border. A wigwam of runner beans of the variety 'Painted Lady', some yellow bush courgettes ('Golden Zucchini') or a group of 'Bull's Blood' beetroot, with their glossy dark purple leaves, would quickly fill an unwelcome gap.

Providing a framework

Vegetables you can train up canes will provide focal points in the border, the obvious one being the scarlet-flowered runner bean, which will run up a bamboo wigwam with little or no help. Pumpkins, gourds, climbing marrows and squashes can be trained up stout tripods if you want instant height; climbing nasturtiums can be mixed in with them for extra colour.

Winter colour and productivity can be lacking in vegetables, so if your potager is predominantly for the kitchen it helps to have an attractive permanent framework. A small area can be made interesting by dividing it up into a pattern of beds, traversed by narrow paths.

Encourage young children to garden by giving them a small, easy-to-work plot in a part of the garden they like. Start the very young on plants that give quick results.

Winter crops

A few vegetables are worth growing in the winter. Leeks are simple to grow and look good well into early spring. The Jerusalem artichoke is a good standby for the long winter months as you can just leave it in place and dig it as you need it; however, be warned that it is extremely invasive.

There are many types of Chinese and Oriental greens and salads that may be lightly stir-fried or eaten raw; they have a spicy taste and many of them are aromatic. With a small range of these you may pick them fresh throughout the year, even in the winter months. The brassicas are a fairly common sight in the winter vegetable garden, but they are often under attack from many pests and so can be disappointing.

However, there are many other simple vegetables that look well slotted in patches in the flower garden. Broad beans, marrows, carrots, maize and endive are all easy, tasty and attractive. The 'cut-and-come again' lettuces, such as the frilly-leaved Lollo Rosso, can be grown throughout the year and help to fill bare patches.

Companion planting

The use of companion planting works particularly well with this style of gardening. *Tagetes patula* (French marigold) will attract hoverflies, which feed on aphids, while nasturtiums secrete a substance into the soil that is absorbed by plants and increases their resistance to certain pests.

I prefer to grow my herbs in my small potager rather than in a herb garden. French or plain-leaved parsley, coriander, lovage, mint, chives, basil, sorrel, tarragon and thyme are planted in individual small squares surrounded by low box hedging so that they can be covered with fleece or glass through the cooler months.

Providing good soil

It is important to keep the soil in a productive garden in good heart so that it is easy to work and will produce healthy plants that will not succumb to pests and diseases. If your soil is on the heavy side, consider having raised beds which can be worked without stepping on them. The sides are usually raised with timber planks or old sleepers, although brick, if the budget allows, can work well.

Attractive and tasty vegetables

Artichoke (globe)
Delicious, easy perennial that germinates well from seed. Sow seed in early spring.

Artichoke (Jerusalem)
A rather invasive but extremely easy perennial that is an ideal plant for providing a fast-growing screen for other vegetables. Plant the tubers in the dormant season. Tubers for eating can be dug up throughout the winter.

Asparagus
A perennial vegetable with attractive ferny foliage that turns butter yellow in autumn; establish for two seasons from crowns (planted in the dormant season) before cutting. Likes free-draining soil.

Beetroot 'Bull's Blood'
This variety has showy, glossy, dark purple leaves but does not form such big roots as less attractive varieties. Sow in mid-spring to early summer.

Cardoon
These stunning perennials can easily be justified for decorative purposes only. If you want to eat them, treat them as annuals. They are easily grown from seed sown in early spring.

Cauliflower 'Purple Queen'
A quick-growing purple-headed cauliflower for autumn; sow late spring to early summer.

Chard 'Ruby Chard'
A variety with intensely coloured leaves of dark purple with a wide red succulent mid-rib. It is easy to grow and very hardy. Sow early spring to early summer.

Climbing French beans 'Gold Marie'
A variety with pale yellow, flat pods and white flowers. It is ideal for training up wigwams and fences. Sow mid-spring to early summer.

Courgette 'Gold Rush'
A rich golden delight, forming a compact bush. Sow late spring to early summer.

Cucumber 'Burpless Tasty Green'
An outdoor variety that is ideal for training up stout wigwams. Plant outside in early summer.

Lettuce 'Lollo Rosso'
An ideal cut-and-come-again lettuce with frilly red leaves. It can be grown throughout the year.

Ornamental cabbage F$_1$ 'Tokyo Mixed'
This is variegated in combinations of two to four colours of purple-pink, green and white. Sow early summer to plant out midsummer.

Ornamental kale 'Peacock Tails'
The purple and crimson leaves make this plant really stand out. It is hardy through the winter, when the colour intensifies. Sow in early summer to plant out midsummer.

Pumpkin 'Hundredweight'
This trailing pumpkin can be trained up stout canes to give height. It produces enormous yellow-skinned fruit. Sow seeds in late spring or early summer.

Radicchio 'Variegata di Sottomarina Precoce'
The leaves are cut-and-come-again and can be eaten cooked or raw. When mature they are an attractive speckled red and white. Sow seeds in late spring to late summer.

Runner beans 'Painted Lady'
This climbing bean has red and white flowers, splendid for tripods or wigwams. Sow in late spring or early summer.

Squash 'Sunburst'
A bright yellow patty pan squash. Plant out in early summer.

GARDEN FURNITURE

Garden furniture is a wonderfully versatile way of adding individuality to a garden design. Available in a vast array of styles, from traditional to modern, rustic to Regency, it sets the style of a garden simply and forcefully.

Using colour

Often, a simple, bold colour scheme for furniture is the most restful. Consider carrying the colour of the furniture through to other hard features such as fencing, gates and doors. If you want to make a seat into a focal point, a white-painted finish that is offset by a dark green hedge will do the trick.

Blue is an underused colour in gardens, but can work beautifully. Dark blue, bold blue, cornflower blue, turquoise-blue and grey-blue can be used to stunning effect on furniture, pots and other paintable surfaces. For people who are not keen on the maintenance aspect of painted furniture, wood stains are an excellent option as the preparation process is easier.

Colour can also be introduced to furniture with fabric – for example, a traditional, wooden deck chair with a bright yellow canvas seat makes a cheerful feature in the garden, or a swing seat draped in a boldly striped canvas cover adds a wonderful splash of colour and is very soothing to sit in. Cushions can also be used to emphasize the colour scheme. Awnings (over a terrace, for example) are another useful way to bring in colour, and can be co-ordinated with fabric on the furniture.

Unusual garden furniture

Almost invariably the most memorable pieces of furniture are purpose-made examples. This may be as simple as a curved bough from an old apple tree made into a simple, half-rounded bench; or as sophisticated as a turf bench supported by bricks and built to form a raised rectangular seat with a clipped box hedge forming the back.

Two round stone balls with a long stone flag over the top make an unusual seat perfectly in keeping with many gardens. Even logs can be fairly easily carved to form interesting shapes and simple seats. And do not forget the all-time favourite resting place – a hammock slung between two trees. This can be double or single and looks attractive both in and out of use.

To add a special finishing touch to any bench, enclose it in an arbour: three parallel hazel wands, each bent to form a wide arch is effective. Interweave short lengths of supple, green hazel into the arch to make it more rigid, then tie it securely with a natural-coloured twine. Festoon it with a fragrant climber, such as an old rose, sweet peas or honeysuckle.

For small children's garden benches, upturned flower pots supporting wooden planks or tree-trunk furniture (see p. 65) are ideal. There is the additional bonus that such items can be moved or grouped together as the children use the area for different activities – from tea parties to a shop.

A suitable outdoor sitting area for young children will be used for play as well as for snacking and chatting.

This eye-catching turf seat, ideally shaped for reclining, was designed by Dan Pearson. It is constructed from marine plywood faced with wood boards, and there are drainage holes in the base to prevent waterlogging. The turf could be replaced with chamomile if you wanted to avoid the need for regular mowing with shears.

On a scorching hot summer's afternoon, the perfect spot to sit is underneath a tree in dappled shade. Tree seats are often made with backs, making them a more comfortable and eye-catching feature, although you need a large, handsome tree to carry it off. Tables around trees can be charming too.

Hammocks must be the simplest and most romantic piece of garden furniture, and they can be enjoyed by all ages. If you are not fortunate enough to have two suitable trees they can be fixed to pergola beams, across a sunny corner of a building, or even between two climber-covered free-standing posts.

GARDEN BUILDINGS

The commonest form of garden building is the shed. This is most frequently a prefabricated utilitarian building at the bottom of the garden and jam-packed with the lawnmower, old newspapers, tools and disused play equipment. These buildings are often best camouflaged with vigorous creepers, and indeed once they are totally covered they can look quite fetching.

If you are buying such a shed remember that it will not be possible to hide it from day one, so make sure you get one with a pitched roof as it is the roof line that makes many sheds look so unsightly. Paint or stain the walls to fit in with your garden. A subtle weathered olive green would help it harmonize with rampant climbers. Alternatively, you could make a statement by painting it with an eye-catching colour such as duck-egg blue, adding a few refinements such as a simple finial over the door and placing large pots of grasses outside.

The siting of your garden building will depend on the prominence you wish it to have. Whatever the building may be, the rules are to site it sympathetically, keep it in tune with the garden, do not be afraid to use colour boldly, and make it as usable and accessible as possible.

Making your own shed

When you are looking for a suitable building, it is easy to become overwhelmed by the range of styles available and the cost. The best examples of garden buildings I have seen are invariably home-made or else especially designed to fit the site. The overall style is the most crucial decision. Make sure that the character of the building you

want will fit in with the garden, and that the colour and materials link in with those used nearby. Be cautious about siting it too prominently – buildings tend to blend in better when there is substantial foliage to anchor them to the garden. Pay particular attention to the roof detail, as it often makes or breaks a building. If you cannot run to the luxury of hand-made reclaimed tiles do not despair – consider cladding it with timber shingles, using an open trellis, thatching it or overlapping bands of stained plywood. The pitch and proportion of the roof are important – try drawing up different angles and sizes before you decide.

Greenhouses

Greenhouses (or glasshouses, as professionals call them) are often eyesores, and as such are best hidden away. This is not easy as they obviously need the light, so cannot be lost among some big bushes like a shed. The best solution is to build one with a wooden frame (painted if you wish), which can last for a long time if properly treated. Design it so that it looks attractive, perhaps with a base of stone or brick. Site the greenhouse with care, remembering that it requires regular attention so a bottom-of-the-garden position is not practical.

This secluded thatched building in its wild setting forms a perfect hideaway and is a great draw to children as a centre for their adventures.

This modern building is adjacent to a pool and a fountain. It is built of well-finished concrete and is on two levels linked by a spiral staircase.

This summerhouse forms the focus of the main sitting area. It can revolve, which means it can be directed to catch (or avoid) the sun throughout the day.

This garden shed with greenhouse can function as a playhouse, a useful storage space and somewhere to sit and relax. It benefits from clever siting and generous planting and fencing.

THE WATER GARDEN

It is rare to see a stunning garden that totally lacks water in one form or other. Water adds a magical quality to an outdoor space, and its diverse qualities allow it to be used to create vastly different moods. According to the nature of the garden, water can effect a delightful transformation, be it a formal well contributing its refreshing coolness to a sunbaked garden, a rushing, 'natural' stream adding speed and excitement to an informal meadow, or a stately fountain providing a classical ambience.

THE APPEAL OF WATER

In the garden, a water feature exerts an almost magnetic pull on adults and children alike. The sound of running water and the visual delight of shallow sparkling water or deep limpid pools encourages us to become absorbed and our mood to become more serene. Interestingly, scientific studies have shown that the negative ions produced by moving water are conducive to a feeling of well-being in people and animals.

From a gardener's point of view, water opens up new horizons, welcoming into the garden a different habitat with its own range of interesting plants, such as dramatic bog plants, floating water plants and a host of marginal aquatic plants. A water habitat also attracts many wild birds and animals of particular interest to children but fascinating for all ages. Ideally, site water where you can view it from the house. Although stark at first, a well-planted water feature can quickly look attractive and well established.

Child safety

Concern about including a water feature in a family garden is understandable. A baby or toddler can drown in the smallest depth of water required to cover his or her nostrils and mouth – a few centimetres. However, by including a safety grid in your pool, small children will be safe should an accident occur (babies and toddlers should be supervised at all times near water). The safety grid is a metal grille that sits about 50mm (2in) below the water surface, allowing water lilies and other water plants to grow through it so that it is scarcely visible. Even if you decide against a water feature initially, include one on your master plan to be added to the garden once the children are bigger.

Simple water features

If you are still worried about the safety implications of having a pool in the garden, simple water features are safer still. Small water features have a quite different charm to larger pools. They particularly appeal to children, who can identify with the small scale and are fascinated by the movement and magic of the water. For example, a bubble fountain makes a lovely focal point, or a shallow, racing well of water running through a garden would be terrific for paddling and racing boats.

Troughs and sinks
One of my favourite gardens has a small stone sink on the terrace filled with water, a few aquatic plants, pebbles, some fish, and a few snails. This could hardly be simpler, and the children love it.

Wall features
Masks on walls with water erupting from their mouths into shallow pools are an old favourite. The water level can be kept very shallow while the children are young by building up the base with heaps of pebbles and sand. Even a piece of pipe coming out of a wall may fit the bill, especially if you disguise it with an abundant climber, such as *Clematis armandii*.

Shallow water channels
These add an element of fun to a garden. They are ideal for sailing small boats in, and cooling hot, sticky fingers.

A large clam-shaped dish filled with pretty pebbles and shells will be enjoyed by small children on hot days as well as being kept in use by birds and other wildlife.

How to make a bubble fountain

It is possible to buy these in kit form, but they are simple to make yourself.

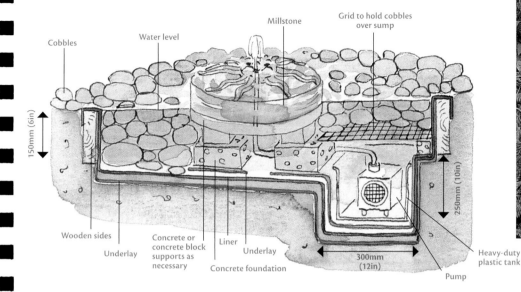

Cobbles

Water level

Millstone

Grid to hold cobbles over sump

150mm (6in)

Wooden sides

Underlay

Concrete or concrete block supports as necessary

Liner

Concrete foundation

Underlay

250mm (10in)

300mm (12in)

Pump

Heavy-duty plastic tank

A tiny water feature such as this will add a charming element to a corner and will also contribute to the play and wildlife value of a garden.

1 Mark out and then excavate the area to a depth of about 150mm (6in). Dig an additional hole for the heavy-duty plastic tank that contains a miniature submersible pump, suitable for giving the lift and flow of water required. An electricity supply will be needed for the pump. Ideally, use a low-voltage pump powered from a transformer inside the house. Call in an electrician to install the wiring.

2 Once the concrete or concrete block foundation is laid, place a butyl liner over the underlay and position the trunk and pump. Place the millstone on its supports and fit the pipework to connect the fountain and pump. Run the supply lead to the pump through a plastic tube, concealed under the cobbles, to protect it from damage. Place a metal grille over the tank, cover it with cobbles and fill to the brim with water. Top up the water level regularly.

Children adore stepping stones and will spend hours playing games on and around them.

PROJECT: A RAISED FORMAL POOL

This pool has an edging of paving slabs, with one side raised above ground in the form of a low brick wall – ideal for sitting on – and the other side flush with the ground. If you have small children, the raised edge provides a small safety barrier although the pool is fitted with a safety grid. The informal pool variation (pp. 86-87) is more natural, with curved lines and soft edging with grass or planting.

Safety and maintenance

The safety grid lies 50mm (2in) below the water level, so that water lilies and other water plants grow through to help mask it. The grid can be removed for thinning the vegetation and general maintenance. It is designed to take a loading of 22kg (50lb) mid-span, but do not allow children to play on it – it is not a play surface.

An overflow is not necessary. However, in the unlikely event of the pool being brimful of water due to very heavy rain, the grid might be 115mm (4½in) below the water surface, thereby increasing the risk to very young children. If the safety risk concerns you, install an overflow.

Check regularly (at least three times a year) that the structure is safe, making sure that the fixings are secure and that any areas of corroding metal or exposed water are dealt with.

You will need

- 28 paving slabs, 450 x 450 x 38mm (18 x 18 x 1½in)
- Heavy-gauge black butyl liner, 5 x 3.8m (16ft 6in x 12ft 6in)
- Underlay, 5 x 3.8m (16ft 6in x 12ft 6in)
- Additional underlay for underplanting and straps, approx. 4.2 x 3m (13ft 9in x 10ft)

- 90 bricks (those positioned at the water's edge must be of paving quality or similar)
- 32 dense concrete blocks, 100 x 225 x 450mm (4 x 9 x 18in)
- Building sand, 0.36m³ (½ cu.yd)
- Concrete, 1:6 (cement:ballast) mix 1m³ (1.3 cu.yd)
- Mortar, 1:4 cement:soft sand mix
- Four square section galvanized steel bars (made by a blacksmith), 1.85m (73in) in length, 20mm (¾in) square, with a 2.5mm (¹⁄₁₆in) wall thickness
- Specially shaped galvanized steel straps, 40mm (1½in) wide by 6mm (¼in) thick, to be welded both ends (see illustration)
- Non-toxic black paint finish (for steel straps)
- Three galvanized steel mesh grids, 1.22 x 1.85m (48 x 73in), with 3mm (⅛in) diameter bars at 50mm (2in) centres, to be painted with a non-toxic black paint finish (the normal sheet size of mesh is 1.22 x 2.44m / 48 x 96in. Ask a blacksmith to cut the sheet to the required size and smooth off all sharp ends)
- Galvanized wire for ties, 1.6mm (¹⁄₁₆in) thick (16 gauge)
- Reinforcing rods for concrete, 12m (40ft) in length, 10mm (⅜in) in diameter

Tools
- Spade or digger • Brick chisel or bolster
- Shovel • Club hammer • Bricklayer's trowel
- Spirit level • Wire cutters • String line
- Sharp knife or scissors

Digging the hole and edge

1 Set out the pool and establish the proposed water level. Dig the hole, incorporating ledges to accommodate marginal plants. The sides of the hole should slope outwards at about 20° (one unit outwards to every three up) to the vertical.

2 Dig out the area that will form the edge treatment. If you are building a raised pool surround, excavate a trench 500mm (20in) below the finished ground level and 525mm (21in) wide. Fill the base of this trench to a depth of 225mm (9in) with concrete. When it has set (allow 48–72 hours), build a 225mm (9in) thick inner wall from the dense concrete blocks, alternate courses being laid flat as shown. Stagger the vertical joints in alternate courses by cutting the end flat blocks in half.

3 The wall will be concealed beneath the liner, so do not point it, but do rub off any projecting mortar to prevent damage to the liner. Using mortar, build the wall to a height of 450mm (18in), putting in butterfly ties spaced at 900mm (36in) centres horizontally and 350mm (14in) centres vertically, to tie in the brickwork wall.

4 Next, build a 100mm (4in) thick brick wall. If preferred, you can substitute stone for the brick, but the facing stone would need to be 200mm (8in) thick and so the coping should be increased accordingly. This brick wall is in stretcher bond (with vertical joints staggered in alternate courses), eight courses high. It is built on the concrete foundation and tied into the block work with the butterfly ties. Use the mortar mix, and the wall should be pointed up. Keep the brickwork straight and vertical by using a string line and spirit level.

5 Excavate about 325mm (13in) below the finished level of the slabs. Lay 100mm (4in) of concrete. It is advisable to put reinforcing rods in the concrete where shown.

Fitting the pool liner

6 When all the mortar and concrete has set, remove the formwork, put a layer of building sand 25mm (1in) over the base of the pool and trowel up the sides with wet sand. Lay the underlay over the sand, bringing it up over the sides, then folding it into the profile made by the partially completed pool surround. Carefully lay the butyl liner over the underlay, folding it into neat gathers.

7 For the raised pool surround, build two courses of 215mm (9in) brickwork (or stone) over the liner, on top of the blockwork wall. These bricks wedge the liner and hide it if the water level drops.

8 For the flush pool surround, lay two courses of 100mm (4in) stretcher bond brickwork over the liner, on top of the concrete. Then bring the liner and underlay up over the back of the brickwork, before laying the next 150mm (6in) depth of

concrete. This brings the concrete base flush with the top of the brickwork. The top of the concrete and brickwork must be level all around the pool. Lay the underlay and liner on top of the concrete when it has set.

Fitting the steel and coping

9 The next stage involves positioning the specially made flat steel straps with the box section steel bars welded to them. The steel straps have a 25mm (1in) 'return' to hook over the brickwork of the raised edge or the concrete of the flush edge, with 215 and 390mm (8½ and 15⅜in) horizontal lengths respectively. The bars span the width of the pool, finishing about 75mm (3in) from both edges. They are placed at 946mm (37¼in) centres, with the end bars 100mm (4in) from the ends. Before positioning them, put an additional layer of underlay over the liner to cushion the metal strap. Check that the bars are level.

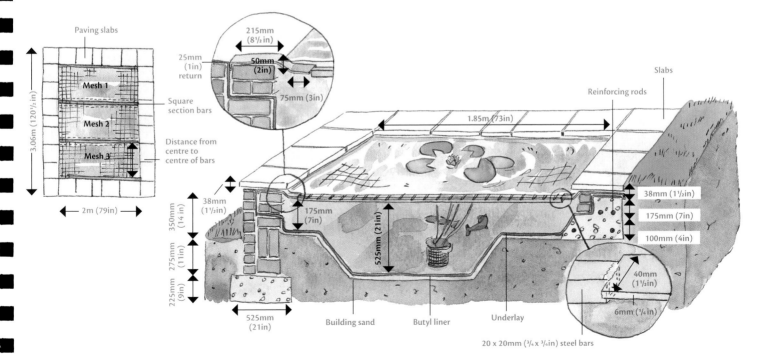

10 Once the bars have been positioned the coping is mortared on top of the strap and liner, with a generous overhang of about 60mm (2½in). Bed each slab on three strips of mortar. Use a spirit level to make sure the surround is level. To include an overflow, lay a 25mm (1in) diameter black PVC pipe in the mortar bed, leaving it just proud of the outside edge.

11 If you are installing a submersible pump or light fittings, lay the cables into the pool in the mortar bed under the coping slabs through a PVC conduit. Low-voltage fittings are powered from a transformer in the house. Call in an electrician to install mains voltage versions.

Planting

12 When the mortar has set, position underlay over the pool base to cushion the liner, carefully weighing it down with bricks. Put a 100–150mm (4–6in) deep layer of good loam soil over the whole base of the pool. Fill the pool, via a double-check valve if using mains water, by resting the end of a hose on the soil in the pool. Keep water pressure to a gentle trickle.

13 First plant the marginal and aquatic plants, then add the oxygenating plants. If you have constructed the pool in winter, wait until spring to plant all but the oxygenating plants. Either plant in top soil in the pool or in aquatic plant containers in appropriate planting compost.

Positioning the steel grids

14 Finally, position the grids over the hollow section steel bars. They must be overlapped

by at least 100mm (4in). Position the outer two grids 25mm (1in) away from the ends of the pool and centre the other grid over the middle two support bars. Tie them in place with galvanized wire, at a maximum of 300mm (12in) centres. Make sure that the ends of the ties are tucked in well.

Variation: **an informal pool**

The illustration opposite shows a cross-section through a typical pool, consisting of the square section metal bars that span 2m (79in) and additional, supporting bricks under the liner. The area between the bricks and the edge is filled with soil and marginal plants. In order to make the pool sufficiently natural and irregular, this distance is best varied, making it 600mm (24in) or more in some places and reducing it to half this in others. As before, the square section metal bars have flat steel straps welded on to the ends which, this time, have no return and are bolted into concrete through a 10mm (⅜in) diameter hole drilled in both ends. The square section bars for this pool are at 1.02m (40in) centres, with the edge bars not more than 100mm (4in) from the water's edge. The dimensions of the pool shown are about 3.2 x 2m (126 x 79in), but these measurements can be altered provided that you neither increase the 2m (79in) span across the pool nor the maximum of 1.3m (51in) centres of the bars.

You will need · · · · · · · · · ·

- Heavy-gauge black butyl liner, 5.7 x 4.2m (18ft 9in x 13ft 9in)
- Underlay, 5.7 x 4.2m (18ft 9in x 13ft 9in), plus additional underlay to cover the liner in planted areas and to create a buffer over

bricks, about 5 x 3.8m (16ft 6in x 12ft 6in)
- Eight bricks
- Building sand to protect liner, 0.6m³ (¾ cubic yard)
- Concrete, 1:6 cement:ballast mix, 0.1m³ (0.13 cu.yd)
- Mortar, 1:5 cement:soft sand mix
- Four 2m (79in) long, 20mm (¾in) square section, galvanized steel bars with a 2.5mm (⅒in) wall thickness, specially made by a blacksmith
- Specially shaped, galvanized steel straps, 40mm (1½in) wide by 6mm (½in) thick, to be welded to both ends with a hole to take a bolt (see illustration)
- Non-toxic black paint
- Two galvanized steel mesh guards, 1.22 x 2m (48 x 79in), with 3mm (⅛in) bars at 50mm (2in) centres
- One galvanized steel mesh guard, 1.22 x 1.8m (48 x 71in) (Ask a blacksmith to cut the sheets to the required size and smooth off all sharp ends. Paint with a non-toxic black paint finish.)
- Eight bolts, 100mm (4in), 10mm (⅜in) In diameter with protective coating
- Eight metal post supports, 600mm (24in) long, to take posts with a base of 75 x 75mm (3 x 3in)
- Galvanized wire for ties, about 1.6mm thick (16 gauge)

Tools
- Spade or digger • Shovel • Club hammer
- Punch for inserting post supports
- Bricklayer's trowel • Wire cutters • Spirit level
- String line • Sharp knife or scissors

Digging out

1 Set out the pool and establish the proposed water level. Dig out the soil to the profiles shown in the illustration. The boundary between the pool and marsh border must be horizontal and 70mm (2¾in) lower than the water level. Set out the positions of the square section bars and dig a hole 400 x 300 x 175mm deep (16 x 12 x 7in) where each bar crosses the marginal boundary; centre the length of the hole on the bar position.

2 Cast concrete 100mm (4in) deep in the holes and, when it has set, lay one brick on each concrete pad using mortar. The bricks must be level 70mm (2¾in) below water level. To provide a smooth base for the liner, add haunching (an angled fillet of mortar) from the top edges of each brick to the edges of its concrete pad.

3 Next position the metal post supports around the edge. The holes in the metal straps must be positioned centrally over the metal post supports, which should be 50mm (2in) above the water level. Having set out this point, drive the metal post supports into the ground accordingly. Check with the metal bars, straps and a level that the positions are correct.

Fitting the pool liner

4 Follow the same process as for the formal pool. The liner should butt up to the top edge of each post support. Once you have finally adjusted it, lay a double layer of underlay over the concealed bricks to prevent the bars from damaging the liner.

5 Fill the tops of the metal post supports with concrete, level them off and reposition the straps with the holes over them. Push the 100mm (4in) bolts through the holes and anchor them into the wet concrete.

Planting

6 The process is the same as for the formal pool except that the water surface area is reduced. Marginals may be established at the water's edge .

7 Finally, the grids can be positioned over the hollow section steel bars and fixed with metal ties every 300mm (12in). They must overlap by a minimum of 100mm (4in). To soften the pool edges, either increase the marginal planting or cut the grid appropriately, making sure that no sharp edges are left.

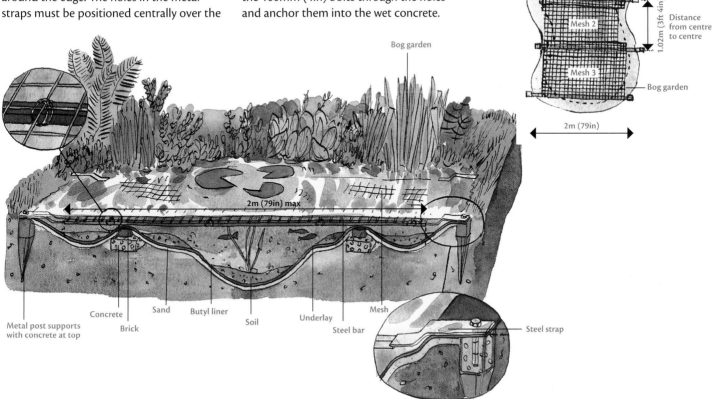

Metal post support

Mesh 1

Mesh 2

1.02m (3ft 4in)

Distance from centre to centre

Mesh 3

Bog garden

2m (79in)

Bog garden

2m (79in) max

Metal post supports with concrete at top

Concrete

Brick

Sand

Butyl liner

Soil

Underlay

Steel bar

Mesh

Steel strap

THE WATER'S EDGE

The edge of a pool is a crucial part of the design. The pool liner should never be revealed – all you should see is the water, the planting and the edging material, if one is used. Many materials can be used to edge water, including bricks, granite setts, boulders, slate, marble, exposed aggregate concrete, timber, pebbles, stone or concrete flags, planting or grass. The important thing is to make sure that the construction detail you use is in harmony with the mood of the area you are creating.

If you are designing a formal pool using a black butyl liner, it is best to finish the vertical face below the coping that is exposed as the water level drops with an attractive surface such as brick or stone (see detail on p. 85). A coping that overhangs by 50–60mm (2–2¾in) will throw the junction of the lining and coping into heavy shadow, so making it very unobtrusive. If the pool is flush with the ground, bring the liner right back under the coping slab and then vertically up at the back, thus allowing the water level to reach the brim that looks more attractive.

Informal pools

Where a pool has an informal edge, it is of equal importance that the black liner does not show. If you are running grass right up to the pool, bring the liner up to form the water's edge at the side of the pool, run it down to a depth of about 200–300mm (8½in) outside the pool, and then bring it back up again. Fill the pocket with soil and cut off the liner at ground level. Plant the pocket of soil with marginal plants, which will butt up against the mown turf.

In the case of a fairly large informal pool the water's edge is often the most intriguing part, so really exploit it. You may want to run a path around the pool, perhaps placing it hard up to the water's edge at one point then snaking it away through an area of boggy planting, perhaps across some stepping stones or a raised wooden walkway.

Poolside features

If you have a poolside building in mind, consider putting it on stilts out in the pool so you can sit almost entirely surrounded by water, able to view the wildlife and watch the water rippling in the breeze. The majority of the base of the building can be on solid ground, with a small area cantilevered out over the water partially supported on stilts. Timber decking can also be cantilevered out over the water for a similar feel.

Pebbles and boulders, which are now readily available in many garden centres, come into their own when used near water.

A gently sloping beach of pebbles can be laid over a butyl liner, creating a natural, attractive edge. Such a beach is excellent for children, as they can wade in gently, and may well be a lifesaver for small mammals, which often drown in straight-sided pools. Clumps of marginals can also be used on these pebbly shores, and areas of sand and gravel can be mixed in too.

Granite setts create an interesting edge detail but must be securely bedded, particularly in a liner pool. The liner should be taken right up behind them.

This simple bridge leads to a similar area of wooden decking that is adjacent to the water's edge. The edge treatment in the foreground consists of horizontal railway sleepers. The flexible liner comes up the inside edge and is concealed by a horizontal hardwood batten that is screwed to the sleeper.

Here a gently sloping area of pebbles at the water side has a wooden decking edge. The shallow slope makes for easy access for frogs, hedgehogs and other animals who use the pond.

Vertical logs contain the edge of the bank. If the pool is made from a flexible liner the fixing should be above it, making the logs mainly cosmetic.

WATER GAMES

Water holds an irresistible allure for children of all ages, and it is not just on hot sunny days that they head for the pool; if it's not warm enough for barefoot paddling they will still enjoy themselves playing pirates, sailing boats or watching the pond life.

The closer to the water children can get the better, so it is worth putting a gently sloping sandy edge in one spot where they can paddle without damaging the liner. A timber structure projecting over the water or a low bridge so that they can sit directly above the water and watch their reflections or drop toys straight in will please them, and stepping stones running over the water are always a firm favourite. A tiny island with restricted access often helps an unnatural water feature to look more natural, provides a refuge for wildlife and stimulates fantasies about castaways.

A source of flowing water will help to increase the oxygen content, so helping to keep the water healthy. It will also provide currents in which to race leaves and toy boats. Even a shallow well racing over coloured gravels with recycled water spurting in at one point will prove a big attraction with youngsters.

Pools within pools

Younger children can be encouraged to create a series of smaller pools within the main pool by making temporary boundaries with small rocks and pebbles; one could be a fish-free zone for rearing young tadpoles, another could be a haven for newts, and a third a protected pool for baby fish to ensure they do not get swallowed up by large hungry relations. Include some small colourful water plants such as *Mimulus guttatus*, *Myosotis scorpioides* and *Typha minima*, the miniature bullrush.

OPPOSITE
This idyllic pastime is not often possible in the average garden, but with larger liner pools now available it is becoming much more achievable.

Children and adults appreciate being able to get right down to the water's edge. If you can create shallows for paddling, they will undoubtedly be well used.

Pooh sticks is a favourite game that can be played wherever there are bridges and running water. Strategic gaps in the waterside planting here allow access for play.

WATER PLANTS

One of the most rewarding tasks in gardening is establishing a water garden, as the plants often grow fast. The best method of establishing aquatic plants is debatable. One system is to place all the rooted plants in plastic containers filled with soil and position them on the floor of the pool; another is to cover the base of the pool with about 150mm (6in) good loam soil with a fine particle size, on top of a layer of underlay to protect the liner.

Unless you have a tiny pre-formed pool, I would always recommend the latter system as the aquatic plants establish in a more natural-looking way. However, you do have to thin them out annually, or whenever they get too crowded. The other system gives you far greater control of the plants, which can be divided as required.

Algae flourish in bright light, so provide shade to prevent them from thriving. You should aim to have about one third of the surface area of the water in shade, and this can be created by free-floating aquatic plants or the foliage of water lilies and other deep-rooted subjects.

Planting

Carry out the planting in mid- to late-spring. Choose a warm day because you will need to get wet! If you have a friend with a well-established pool, offer to help thin out the plants, and with luck you might get some pond snails and water boatmen too. If you are using container plants from a garden centre, planting can be done at any time of year.

The oxygenators – submerged rooted plants such as *Ceratophyllum demersum* (hornwort) and *Potamogeton crispus* (curly pondweed) – are vital to a good water balance, which results in clear water without the use of chemicals. Plant them by pushing the ends into the soil and wedging with a rock or brick.

Plant the other types of rooted plants in a similar way, wedging them down with bricks or stones where necessary. It is much more rough and ready work than putting in a border plant – you do it very fast, partly because your hands start to freeze and also because that is all that is required. The floating plants just need placing – it could not be easier.

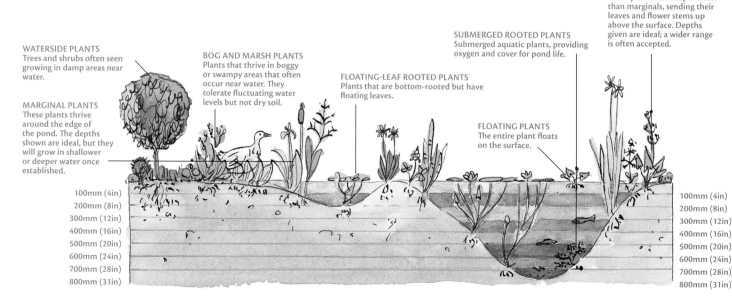

WATERSIDE PLANTS
Trees and shrubs often seen growing in damp areas near water.

MARGINAL PLANTS
These plants thrive around the edge of the pond. The depths shown are ideal, but they will grow in shallower or deeper water once established.

BOG AND MARSH PLANTS
Plants that thrive in boggy or swampy areas that often occur near water. They tolerate fluctuating water levels but not dry soil.

FLOATING-LEAF ROOTED PLANTS
Plants that are bottom-rooted but have floating leaves.

SUBMERGED ROOTED PLANTS
Submerged aquatic plants, providing oxygen and cover for pond life.

FLOATING PLANTS
The entire plant floats on the surface.

EMERGENT PLANTS
These plants like deeper water than marginals, sending their leaves and flower stems up above the surface. Depths given are ideal; a wider range is often accepted.

100mm (4in)
200mm (8in)
300mm (12in)
400mm (16in)
500mm (20in)
600mm (24in)
700mm (28in)
800mm (31in)

100mm (4in)
200mm (8in)
300mm (12in)
400mm (16in)
500mm (20in)
600mm (24in)
700mm (28in)
800mm (31in)

Planting positions for water plants

Name	Depth	Comments	N = native or commonly naturalized
Waterside trees and shrubs			
Alnus glutinosa (common alder)		Establishes and grows very fast; useful on poor subsoils. Height 20m (65ft). **N**	
Comus alba 'Sibirica' (dogwood)		Striking red stems, which need cutting back every other year to keep the vibrant colour. Height 3m (10ft).	
Salix x *chrysocoma* (weeping willow)		The ideal natural den. Height 12m (40ft).	
Salix viminalis (common osier)		Use the shoots and young branches to weave a willow den. Height 3m (10ft). **N**	
Viburnum opulus (guelder rose)		Eye-catching flowers and berries, a most attractive native plant. Height 3m (10ft). **N**	
Bog and marsh plants			
Gunnera manicata		This magnificent large-leaved plant up to 2m (6ft) high adds a tropical feel to damp areas.	
Ligularia dentata 'Desdemona'		A dramatic plant up to 1.2m (4ft) high with purple-black stems and vivid orange daisy-like flowers.	
Petasites japonicus var. *giganteus*		This plant can be invasive but is useful for colonizing large areas. Height to 1.5m (5ft).	
Primula florindae		A stunning plant similar to a giant cowslip, which will naturalize in damp zones. Try planting with *P. japonica* 'Miller's Crimson'. Height up to 1m (3ft).	
Marginal plants			
Caltha palustris (marsh marigold)	0–150mm (0–6in)	Attractive yellow flowers. **N**	
Iris pseudacorus (yellow flag)	0–250mm (0–10in)	Vigorous, with eye-catching yellow flowers. **N**	
Lysimachia nummularia (creeping jenny)	0–50mm (0–2in)	Creeping plant with bright golden flowers. **N** The yellow-leaved form *L n.* 'Aurea' is more striking.	
Lysichiton americanus (skunk cabbage)	0–300mm (0–12in)	Bold leaves followed by bright arum-shaped flowers.	
Mentha aquatica (water mint)	0–200mm (0–2in)	Vigorous plant with lilac flowers and a strong minty aroma. **N**	
Mimulus luteus (monkey musk)	30–150mm (1¼–6in)	Splendid yellow flowers with maroon and brown spots.	
Myosotis scorpioides (water forget-me-not)	0–150mm (0–6in)	Has small clusters of bright blue flowers that will flower again if cut back early. **N**	
Zantedeschia aethiopica 'Crowborough' (arum lily)	0–250mm (0–10in)	A very striking plant with large glossy arrow-shaped leaves and beautiful white flowers.	
Emergent plants			
Butomus umbellatus (flowering rush)	30–250mm (1–10in)	Extremely pretty rosy-pink flowers produced in umbels in early to midsummer. **N**	
Menyanthes trifoliata (bog bean)	50–300mm (2–12in)	This spreading plant looks rather like broad beans and has white flowers tipped with pink. **N**	
Orontium aquaticum (golden club)	25–400mm (10–16in)	Velvety bluish-green leaves, silvery beneath. Curious yellow flowers appear on white stems.	
Sagittaria sagittifolia (arrowhead)	50–400mm (2–16in)	This plant has arrow-shaped leaves and survives in still and flowing water. **N**	
Typha latifolia (lesser reedmace)	50–300mm (2–12in)	Smaller relative of *T. angustifolia* (bullrush). Has brown velvety flower spikes; sparrows enjoy the seed heads. **N**	
Submerged rooted plants			
Callitriche autumnalis (crystalwort)	50–600mm (2–24in)	This plant is useful in the autumn and winter as it grows well beneath ice, contributing a fresh, brilliant green, yet can also cope with seasonal drought. **N**	
Ceratophyllum demersum (hornwort)	300mm–3m (1–10ft)	A dark green semi-floating plant with brittle, much-branched stems. **N**	
Elodea canadensis (Canadian pondweed)	150mm–2m (6in–7ft)	A very aggressive plant, so use with care – do not introduce to ponds that will be left untended as it will be too invasive. Excellent for deep water. **N**	
Potamogeton crispus (curly pondweed)	150–600mm (6–24in)	This plant is at its best in winter and spring when the translucent bronzy-green foliage is evident, before disintegrating in midsummer.	
Floating-leaf rooted plants			
Nymphaea alba (white waterlily)	300mm–3m (1–10ft)	Blooms 10–150mm (4–6in) across, probably too big for most ponds, but wonderful where space allows. **N**	
Nuphar lutea (common pond lily)	500mm–3m (20in–10ft)	A vigorous plant that will tolerate running water and heavy shade. It has bright yellow flowers 40–50mm (½–2in) across with a strong alcoholic smell. Rather rampant so not ideal for garden ponds. **N**	
Nymphoides peltata (fringed waterlily)	100–750mm (4–30in)	Small, bright green leaves and clear yellow-fringed flowers. Suitable for smaller ponds.	
Ranunculus aquatilis (water crowfoot)	100–600mm (4–24in)	Attractive, buttercup-like white flowers with yellow centres appear in spring.	
Floating plants			
Azolla filiculoides (fairy moss, water fern)		This attractive fern changes colour from pale green to rusty red in late summer in full sun. Do not let it cover all the pool as it will prevent oxygen from reaching the water. **N**	
Eichhornia crassipes 'Major' (floating water hyacinth)		Beautiful hyacinth-like flowers. Remove to frost-free quarters in autumn.	
Lemma minor (duckweed)		Many will pay to get this plant removed, but in certain places it looks the part. **N**	
Stratiotes aloides (floating water soldier)		This fascinating plant resembles the cut-off top of a pineapple. The foliage in young plants is a reddish-bronze colour. **N**	

WATER MAINTENANCE

When you are establishing a pond the ideal is to create a healthy natural balance that to a certain extent will regulate itself. However, most garden ponds are not natural. They have no constant supply of water and need topping up from time to time, probably with water from a treated source. This is likely to be relatively rich in nutrients and may cause the algae to proliferate. Top up frequently rather than putting in large quantities at once.

Controlling the vegetation

Aquatic plants are often astonishingly robust and will need tackling about once a year, otherwise they will eventually cover any water less than 1.8m (6ft) deep. Oxygenators, particularly ones such as *Elodea canadensis* (Canadian pondweed) and *Myriophyllum spicatum* (spiked water milfoil), will need thinning out once or even twice a year. In spring, any marginal and emergent plants that are becoming overwhelming will also need to be divided, thinned or cleared.

In spring and/or autumn dead stems and leaves of plants can be cut down and removed, and the growth tidied up. If you have fish in the pool this is better done in autumn as a higher concentration of decomposing matter releases undesirable gases in the water. If there are many trees nearby, you should remove excessive fallen leaves from the bottom of the pool.

Once the pool has become established you may find an algal bloom of blanket weed occurs. A simple way of combating this and many other forms of algae is to sink some barley straw, which, when it rots, releases algal inhibitors (other types of straw are not so effective).

Winter maintenance

During winter place a soft rubber ball in a straight-sided pool to prevent the expanding action of ice cracking the sides. If you have fish, do not let the water freeze over for more than a week as this could harm them. Install a heater, cover a small section to stop it freezing or melt the ice with warm bottles. Do not use a hammer to crack ice as shock waves will damage pond life.

There should be no need to empty the pond out and clean it, and indeed this would be detrimental to the wildlife. However, you may find that the amount of sediment at the bottom builds up, in which case try removing a few buckets of mud in early autumn before the water creatures have begun to hibernate.

Consult your pump supplier to see what treatment is recommended with respect to draining the system. In the case of submersible pumps the advice is usually to run them every other week for just a few minutes to keep them ticking over.

This green slime is blanket weed, which sometimes occurs during the warmer months. It is a natural response to extra fertility, but if it takes over it can reduce the available oxygen.

In this small pool the plants are in containers, limiting the vigorous varieties that would otherwise colonize the entire pool. In larger pools a more natural effect is gained by planting directly into soil on the pool base.

Water problems and solutions

Problem	Solution
Loss of water through evaporation	Top up the water level regularly. If using chlorinated water, never add more than a quarter of the total volume at a time.
Loss of water through leaks	Most liners can be repaired. Drain the water to the level of the leak (removing fish, etc. if necessary), find the leak and patch up.
Cloudy water, usually caused by: i) Not enough oxygenating plants ii) Too much sunlight on water iii) Disturbance of very fine silty or clay soils on bottom by large fish iv) Water balance has not yet had time to establish	i) Add more oxygenating plants. ii) Put in additional plants such as water lilies to create shade. iii) Remove silt or stabilize it by adding a gravel layer on top. iv) Be patient, allow time to let the natural balance establish – this may take a growing season.
Loss of fish to predators such as herons, gulls, kingfishers and cats	Add plants with large floating leaves such as water lilies for cover and/or place a trip wire about 450mm (18in) high around the pond to deter birds such as herons that fish from the water's edge.
Fish gasping for oxygen in hot summers	Give short-term relief by letting water sprinkle over pool surface. For a long-term solution, add more oxygenating, plants, or some water circulation device such as a pump and fountain.
Ice over pool	In winter the expanding action of ice can cause straight-sided pools to crack, so float a soft ball on the surface to relieve the pressure. If there are fish in the pool and the water surface is frozen for a week or more, make one or two holes to allow toxic gases to escape. Do not smash the ice, as this will damage fish and amphibians; instead, place a plastic bottle filled with hot water on the ice, refilling as necessary. Alternatively, place a purpose-built heater in the water, or cover a small area with some insulation.
Fish dying in cold weather	This may be caused by feeding when the water temperature is below 15°C (60°F), in which case the food will decompose in the fish before their metabolism (which slows down in winter) can break it down. Do not feed fish unless water is above this temperature.
Overcrowded and overgrown aquatic plants	Partially clear areas of plants where they are becoming too invasive. Leave discarded plants by the pool for long enough to allow pond life to crawl back to the water. Divide water lilies up when leaves start standing proud of the water and replant giving a good feed of water lily pellets or balls of bonemeal mixed with soil, buried in the compost.
Blanket weed (*Cladophora*) over surface of pool	Sink some barley straw, which will release algae inhibitors and also increase the invertebrate population, some of which will feed on the algae. Put the barley straw in an old onion bag or other netting. It is important that the straw is well aerated, which is to say not too tightly packed together – the recommended rate is 50g per m³ (1½ oz per cu yd). Anchor it just below the surface or near an inflow or fountain. After one to four months your blanket weed problem should disappear. This is best carried out in the spring, before significant problems with algae have had a chance to build up and become entrenched in your pool.

A Garden for Wildlife and Pets

The pleasure that children derive from animals is enhanced by a more relaxed approach to gardening; just mowing the lawn a little higher, leaving seed heads on plants through the winter and keeping some of your dead logs and debris instead of tidying everything away will immediately make the garden more desirable to wildlife. Pet-lovers will also appreciate well-designed pet hutches that house the animal handsomely without detracting from the garden's beauty.

THE WILDLIFE GARDEN

Many gardeners are adapting their plots to make them more sympathetic towards the needs of wildlife. A wildlife garden does not have to be a formless wilderness – it can be designed to cater for the family's needs just like any garden. The main difference is that to encourage wildlife you aim to provide a range of habitats, and when it comes to maintenance you give the requirements of wildlife preference over a tidy appearance.

This may involve, for example, leaving dead flower heads on many plants so that birds and insects can feed on them through the winter. Instead of cutting your herbaceous plants to the ground at the end of the growing season, leave most of them intact to allow insects to inhabit the hollow stems. A pile or two of dead logs in a quiet place is an ideal habitat for various fungi, amphibians and many insects, which in turn will attract hedgehogs, thrushes, wrens and blackbirds.

Choosing plants

Another difference between a wildlife garden and a more conventional garden is the range of plants you choose to grow; ideally you should plant 60–70 per cent native species. Native plants will generally be a host to all sorts of mildews, insects and viruses and will tolerate them quite happily and unobtrusively, whereas a cultivated plant may require a spray that will slaughter every insect around. Although you may not find insects the most glamorous of visitors to your garden, they are a vital part of the food chain. You will be more likely to attract the more lovable forms of wildlife if you have a varied and prolific range of them.

Even in a small urban garden you will be able to re-create many wildlife habitats such as woodland, wildflower meadows, pool and wetland. A woodland edge surrounding the garden can be planted to provide privacy and shelter, and may contain shrubs and a few native trees underplanted with bluebells, primroses and foxgloves. A mown path could meander through a flowering meadow bordering a natural-looking pond. A long grass and wild flower meadow has the added advantage of requiring less maintenance than a traditional lawn.

A wildlife garden has a smaller proportion of evergreens than a conventional garden, and other factors such as berries and seedpods take precedence. Bear wildlife in mind when you are doing any work in the garden. Try to lay your paving on sand rather than concrete so insects can live underneath; provide a generous bird-feeding area out of the way of the local cats; raise the height of your lawnmower blades about 25mm (1in) and your lawn will be far more attractive for insects and the grass will become increasingly invaded by wild flowers. Try to reduce the amount of weedkillers, insecticides and fungicides you use, using them as a last resort.

Foxgloves provide a wonderful woodland edge effect and are one of the simplest plants to grow from seed. They have a charming trait of coming up in places where it would be impossible to plant them.

Attracting wildlife

Bear wildlife in mind when you are working in the garden, such as planting flowers that attract bees, which will in turn attract birds and mammals.

Foxes

Urban foxes are predominantly nocturnal. Putting out pet food at the same time each day will encourage them to return. Occasionally, they occupy the area beneath garden sheds and they also like dense shrubbery.

Birds

Many of our favourite garden birds nest in hollow tree trunks or holes in rotten branches. Nesting boxes make a good alternative – camouflage them well, put them out of direct sun, and provide several with different-sized holes. Put up a bird table that provides food at different levels for different types of feeders. A constant water source is vital.

Ladybirds

Apart from their pretty spotted appearance (there are some 45 species in England), ladybirds are useful to have in your garden as both the adult

and the immature larvae will eat through vast quantities of greenfly, blackfly and other pests. To encourage them, make an insect hibernator (see right) by fixing a panel of hollow stems of various sizes to a wall.

Hedgehogs

Hedgehogs enjoy a diet rich in slugs, snails and insects, so a heap of decaying wood provides a good hedgehog diner. Do not set fire to heaps of vegetation in autumn and winter without checking for the presence of hibernating hedgehogs. Never leave out bread and milk – milk upsets their digestion and encourages infection. Tinned dog food is the best alternative.

Bats

Several of our insect-eating native species of bat are threatened with extinction, so count yourself lucky if you can watch bats hunting for food on a calm summer evening; growing night-scented flowers and leaving an outside light on at dusk will attract moths and other night-flying insects that form a major food source. Put up a bat box on a sheltered, quiet wall or tree, train climbers against battens fixed to a wall or fence or build a dry-stone wall 'rockery' with cavities that will house their prey as well as the bats themselves.

A WILDLIFE GARDEN PLAN

This is very much a family garden, designed to include the requirements of three gregarious teenagers aged between ten and sixteen.

A wide terrace next to the modern house is continually used for eating and entertaining, and has large glazed doors and windows that look over the water to the garden house. From here a bird-feeding station can also be observed.

The garden house

The walls are made from woven willow branches with layers of wet loam combined with straw thrown against the willow frame. The sun baked the walls hard and a lime wash was then applied inside and out, purely for aesthetic purposes. There are bat and bird boxes built into the house, and the floor is wooden in the hope that a fox might make an earth beneath it. A short stretch of curving stone wall leading from the house has larger holes at the bottom that form tempting dank refuges for toads.

The wetland area

The water has marshy areas around it that seethe with wildlife. To give more timid occupants shelter, the area between the pool and fence has only limited accessibility. A boardwalk projecting over the water is frequently used by the children. This area is very visible from the house, and as such is easy for the parents to monitor and provides a continual source of interest.

The woodland area

A mown grass path meanders from the much-used large paved area past the pool on to a tiny 'woodland' area. In a small glade a circular turf bank contains a large sand pit. The area under the trees has longer grass studded with wild flowers. The trees support hammocks, ropes, swings and platforms and shelter small encampments. This area provides nectar, seeds, fruits, foliage and accommodation for insects, mammals and amphibians.

The vegetable garden

The vegetable garden is separated by a willow fence, covered in summer with runner beans, climbing nasturtiums and sweet peas. The stones and boulders are really there to provide a home for lizards and insects, but are repeatedly disturbed by the children using them as building materials for some new project or other. A pile of decaying wood is home to myriad insects, amphibians and fungi.

This small edible fungi garden has been made from a selection of rotting logs that had their top surface and sides scored and fixed with damp rotting straw and fungal spores.

Put up a variety of bird boxes even in the smallest garden to provide safe nesting places for a range of birds from blue tits to owls.

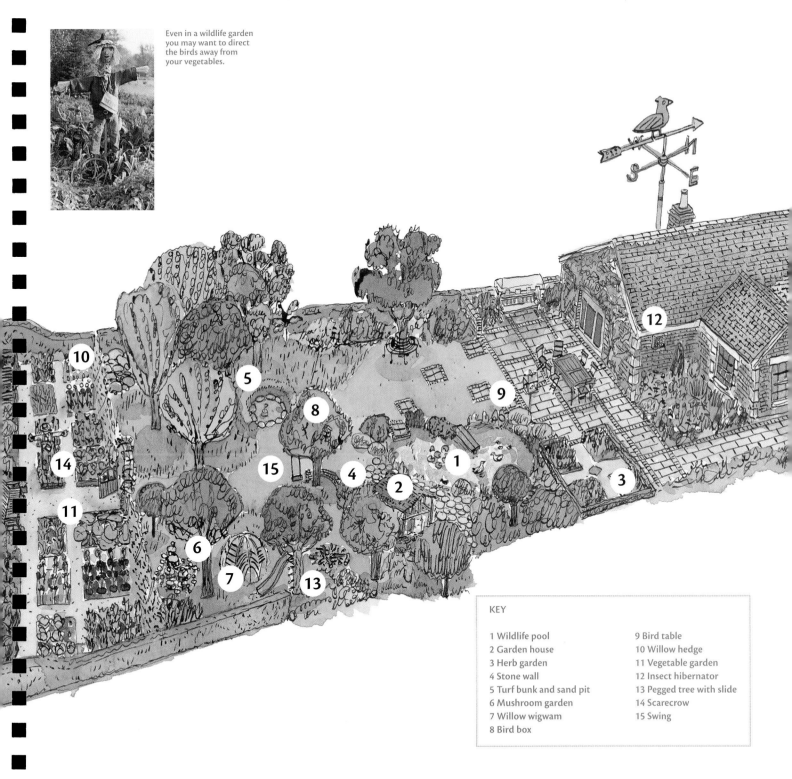

Even in a wildlife garden you may want to direct the birds away from your vegetables.

KEY

1 Wildlife pool
2 Garden house
3 Herb garden
4 Stone wall
5 Turf bunk and sand pit
6 Mushroom garden
7 Willow wigwam
8 Bird box

9 Bird table
10 Willow hedge
11 Vegetable garden
12 Insect hibernator
13 Pegged tree with slide
14 Scarecrow
15 Swing

WILDFLOWER AND WETLAND HABITATS

Both wildflower and wetland habitats are rapidly disappearing in the countryside, so creating one in your garden will help to support the threatened species of flora and fauna.

The wildflower meadow

Growing wild flowers amid long grass is a relaxing form of gardening that can take as much or as little time as you wish; the basic requirement is only one or possibly two cuts a year. If you are tidy-minded you will have to take a firm hold of yourself during July, once the main show of flowers is over, and wait for your tousled meadow to set seed – only then can you get out the scythe; otherwise you will have a meagre show the following year.

Grow several different patches of flowering meadow to broaden the attraction for local wildlife and keep interest throughout the year:

- Meadow: *Centaurea* spp. (knapweed), *Malva moschata* (musk mallow), *Knautia arvensis* (field scabious), *Silene vulgaris* (bladder campion), *Tanacetum vulgare* (tansy)
- Spring bulbs and early-flowering plants: *Ajuga reptans* (bugle), *Primula veris* (cowslip), *Bellis perennis* (daisy), *Cardamine pratensis* (lady's smock), *Hypochoeris radicata* (cat's ear)
- Late-flowering meadow: *Malva moschata* (musk mallow), *Salvia pratensis* (meadow clary), *Centaurea cyanus* (cornflower), *Knautia arvensis* (field scabious) can be mown until early summer and again in early to mid-autumn.

Many people report a poor success rate when they try to establish wild flowers from seed. This is probably because perennial wild flowers tend not to flower in the first season after germinating. Some of the flowering annuals are best suited to regularly disturbed land and some seeds only germinate if they are very fresh or have had several winters' worth of cold weather.

If you do decide to use seed, your success rate will increase if you sow the seeds into seed trays of potting compost in late summer, and plant them on into small plant pots when they have three or four leaves. Plant them out in their final position the following autumn, 12 months later, watering well until established.

If you are starting your meadow from scratch, let all the weeds present germinate and then remove them. Next sow the grass seed in late summer, then oversow this with a wildflower mixture of your choice. Rake the seed over and firm the seedbed. Water if conditions are dry, but be careful not to wash all the seed out. More precious plants can be planted in small plugs the next autumn when the meadow has established.

Mown paths and edges allow you within easy reach of the various flowers and grasses and also form neater edges to these less structured parts of the garden.

The wetland habitat

Creating a wildlife pool with a surrounding area of wetland is one of the most enthralling tasks in gardening, and as soon as it is finished all sorts of wildlife will start to colonize it. To enjoy your water to the full, site it where it can be observed from the house, allowing the sunlight to fall on it from the south at least. Try to make the pool in proportion to the site, opting for a generous size if you can. See pp. 86-87 for instructions on making a small informal pool with a liner.

After filling the pool, you can start to plant it up in the spring. In that first season, as the plants and aquatic animals start to colonize the water, you will find that it quickly turns a startling spinach green and given good weather may well maintain this lurid colour all summer. Do not be tempted by chemicals and electronic filters, but watch the natural balance start to take over and gradually clear the water as long as you have adequate oxygenating plants – one plant per 300 sq mm (12 sq in) of surface water is recommended, preferably of different varieties. Include some water snails and grey water fleas (*Daphnia*), which eat algae and so help to clear the water.

Two of my favourite waterside plants that seem particularly attractive to wildlife are *Eupatorium cannabinum* (hemp agrimony) and *Ajua reptans* (bugle), loved by butterflies and bees respectively. Both thrive in damp spots, so if you have a liner pool on free-draining soil you will have to create a boggy area beside it.

To make a boggy area, dig out the area required (a minimum of 1–2m²/11–22 sq ft) to a minimum depth of 300mm (12in) or a good 600mm (2ft) if you want to include some of the larger exotic plants, and line it with heavy-gauge polythene. Puncture a few small holes in it and fill it up with a good loam. Some of my favourite boggy plants are the candelabra primulas and *P. japonica* 'Miller's Crimson'. The ornamental rhubarb *Rheum palmatum* makes a great statement and is easy to grow.

To many gardeners one of the attractions of a pool is to watch the fish. For a true wildlife pool, leave out goldfish, which eat vast quantities of frogspawn and tadpoles, and settle for a few stickleback, provided the pool is large enough, and maybe one or two tench to help eat some of the debris in the bottom.

This small marshy area and pool provide a little wetland area. Frogs, toads, newts, dragonflies, water snails and other varieties of wildlife arrived very soon after it was constructed.

From lawn to wildflower meadow

Autumn

1 Reduce soil fertility by removing patches of turf and topsoil about 300 x 300mm (12 x 12in) and replacing with weed-free subsoil.

2 Put in the plants (not seeds), keeping to one type of plant in each patch. Include *Chrysanthemum leucanthemum* (ox-eye daisy), which is an easy starter. Water the plants in until they become established. Planting may also be done in early spring.

3 Put in spring-flowering bulbs, such as *Narcissus pseudo-narcissus* (native daffodil), *Fritillaria meleagris* (snake's head fritillary), *Scilla nutans* (English bluebell), *Tulipa sylvestris* (wild tulip) and *Galanthus nivalis* (snowdrop), depending on conditions.

Spring

Remove any pernicious plants such as nettles, dock or creeping thistle by hand. Carry on doing this throughout the growing season. (If your meadow has a high proportion of these and/or coarse grasses at the outset, remove them by tight mowing for a year prior to introducing the wild flowers.)

Mid- to late-summer

When the flowers have set seed, cut the grass to about 75mm (3in). Leave the 'hay' for a week or two so the seeds drop into the meadow, then remove it to maintain a low soil fertility.

Mid- to late-autumn

Carry out the final cut, removing the cuttings before the spring bulbs start pushing through the turf. This cut ensures that they do not have too much competition.

WOODLAND AND COPPICE

A patch of woodland, even if it is only a strip some 3m (10ft) wide, introduces a mysterious shady quality into part of your garden. It also enables you to provide a multi-tiered woodland edge, bringing in a versatile range of habitats for plants and animals. Do not be put off by the expense or the need for patience – the most successful type of tree planting uses two- to three-year-old transplants (not costly standards) and it is worth waiting for five years or so to reap such rich rewards.

Dense tree and shrub planting has many other benefits, too. It provides shelter, which hastens the growth of all the plants by creating a warmer, kinder micro-climate; it screens out eyesores and diverts the attention to attractive elements; and for children it provides a tough environment where they can climb, swing and hide, as well as concealing items such as climbing frames and swings.

Planting for quick results

You will probably want to encourage a wide range of invertebrates, birds, mammals both large and small, and amphibians, so you will need to provide rich habitats at different levels, trying to keep to predominantly native species. If you are starting from scratch and lack patience, the use of a 'nurse' crop of quick-growing species is essential. Choose trees such as *Betula pendula* (birch) or *Acer campestre* (field maple) that will tolerate exposed windy sites, grow fast and so provide a more sheltered environment for the slower-growing species, such as oak, beech or ash, which will eventually form the backbone of your wood. If you do not

have enough space to accommodate such large trees, go for a closely planted group of smaller native trees such as *Ilex aquafolium* (holly), *Corylus avellana* (hazel) or *Prunus padus* (bird cherry).

One of the most important factors in getting trees to establish fast is choosing the right tree for the soil. On our very free-draining, thin, limestone soil, wild cherry does extremely well. On damp soil I would opt for alders, as these tolerate degrees of wetness that no other tree apart from willow can stand and grow very fast.

The shrub layer

The shrub layer contributes greatly to the shady, enclosed character required and can be used to screen out unwanted views. An informal boundary of native shrubs such as *Rosa canina* (dog rose), *Viburnum opulus* (guelder rose) and *Ligustrum vulgare* (wild privet) will provide a rich habitat and additional shelter, colour and shadow. Throughout your woodland patch, intersperse other groups of native shrubs like hazel, holly or box and use them to help define a woody walk.

This path through young woodland has been surfaced with bark, a sympathetic and economical material that is ideal both for children's demands and for general use.

Management

When the mixed planting has started to produce the form you want and plants are becoming overcrowded, you can start to manicure the woodland. Coppicing – repeatedly cutting trees or shrubs down to ground level – means that sunlight is let in and new plants will establish themselves in those open patches. Many trees can be coppiced, especially hazel, ash, sweet chestnut, birch and willow. If you coppice a few trees after 8–12 years, then coppice a different batch two years later when the growth has thickened up, you will maintain the overall habitat. About eight years after you started, repeat the cycle.

Do not forget the lower storey, where you can plant foxgloves, *Silene dioica* (red campion), *Polygonatum multiflorum* (Solomon's seal) and *Hyacinthoides non-scriptus* (bluebell) as soon as there is enough shade to inhibit the growth of grass.

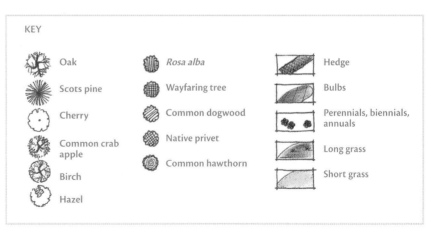

KEY

- Oak
- Scots pine
- Cherry
- Common crab apple
- Birch
- Hazel
- *Rosa alba*
- Wayfaring tree
- Common dogwood
- Native privet
- Common hawthorn
- Hedge
- Bulbs
- Perennials, biennials, annuals
- Long grass
- Short grass

In this small woodland area, trees are planted at a minimum of 1.5m (5ft) centres for quick results. This area is about 10m (32ft) wide by 5m (16½ft) long. The section line AA is shown in detail overleaf.

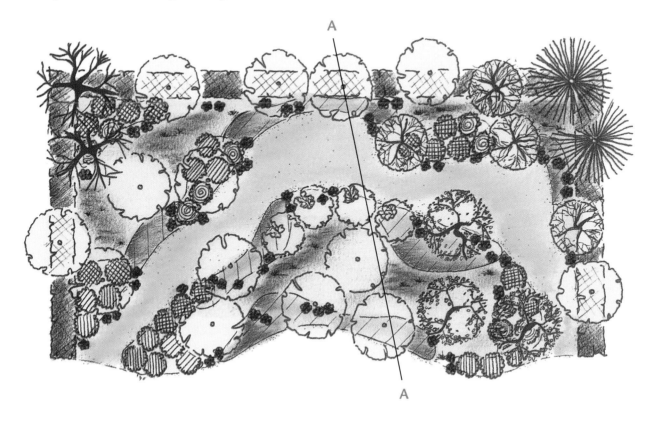

A

A

ESTABLISHING A WOODLAND GARDEN

Once you have chosen the plants for your woodland garden, you have to decide exactly how you are going to establish them. If you are going to plant a native mixed hedge border (see p. 108) or a coppice along the lines of that on p. 105 in an area of existing grass, you will first need to mark out on the ground the positions of the tree and hedge planting, using canes and string. This will help you to visualize your garden and allow you to make any adjustments to your design before you start digging.

Planting trees

To obtain the quick results usually required you must plant the trees approximately 2m (6½ft) apart. For a natural effect the spacing should vary somewhat – maybe 1m (3¼ft) in one place and 3m (10ft) elsewhere. This may seem close, but in 10 years or so you can start to thin them out if required.

As to the size of tree to plant, the smaller the better. Bare-rooted transplants of 450–600mm (1½–2ft) high are extremely cheap and will establish far quicker than a large standard. The established appearance of these smaller trees is more natural, as the major upset given to transplanted standards alters the final form and shape. The maximum size I would use is 1.2m (4ft).

In the first few growing seasons the predominant factor influencing your trees' growth is moisture, so forget the fertilizer initially - just make sure that they have enough to drink. It is often not feasible to water trees, but as long as you ensure that no weeds or grass are growing around the base of their stems to compete for moisture they will probably be fine. If you grow trees with mown grass around their trunks during establishment (the first three or four years) their growth rate will be 60–70 per cent slower than those grown with bare earth around their roots, simply because they are obtaining less water.

A painless way to remove weed competition is to put a tree spat around the base of the tree when planting. These are 450–900cm (1½–3ft) squares of thick black polythene, polypropylene, bituminous felt or wool matting, which are anchored by digging in the corners. They can also be obtained in long runs for hedges. A 50–75mm (2–3in) thick layer of very coarse bark mulch could be used instead, but all perennial weeds would have to be removed first. If you have no objections to using chemicals, apply a non-selective, non-residual, systemic weedkiller to a 1m (3¼ft) diameter patch around the site where the tree will be planted or along entire hedge runs.

1–3 years: Plant small transplants and protect them from rabbits with spiral guards. Keep the ground around the base free of grass and weeds to reduce competition for moisture.

7–10 years: The trees will be producing light shade, so start to introduce wild flowers and ground cover. Remove vigorous weeds if they become a problem.

Rabbits like to gnaw young bark, killing the tree. To prevent this, put plastic spiral tree guards around the base, an easy and inexpensive procedure. Some trees dislike exposure, and individual shelters (usually made from heavy polythene and mesh) can be put round them to assist their growth initially.

Planting the understorey

Once your trees and shrubs are established (3–4 years) moisture competition is not as critical. This is the time to introduce the understorey. You may decide to have no grass apart from mown pathways, which over the years will get shaded out and could then be replaced by bark. Sheets of *Hedera* (ivy), interspersed with patches of *Primula vulgaris* (common primrose), *Anemone nemorosa* (wood anemone), *Allium ursinum* (wild garlic), *Convallaria majalis* (lily-of-the-valley) and ferns are just a few of the available plants that will make your woodland look authentic; a wildflower catalogue will guide your choice. Position your plants in the shadier spaces, control the competition and let them spread with the shade.

Managing the woodland

When you are managing the woodland, keep long-term aims in view. Your ultimate goal is unlikely to be a single-species copse with tall, straight-trunked trees as required for timber production, but rather an area of dappled shade with some character and charm. Maybe you will train a tree to grow at a leaning angle or bend two over to form an archway.

When thinning the trees, you may decide to pull out a perfect example with a single, strong leader and keep a forked specimen instead so that you can fit a tree house into it in a few years.

15–20 years: At this point you may want to thin out some trees. Characterful trees with bent trunks add to the woodland's charm.

HEDGES AND BORDERS

A common choice of plants for hedging is a line of non-indigenous conifers to form a dense boundary. However, a native hedgerow composed of a range of plants to suit the conditions such as hawthorn, viburnum, native privet, holly and dog rose will support an infinitely greater variety of wildlife. It will also provide colour and interest with berries, flowers, budding shoots and autumn leaves, not to mention the scores of plants that will thrive along the hedgerow base.

The visual screen the hedgerow will provide during the summer can be every bit as good as that given by conifers as well as looking a good deal more in harmony with the landscape. If you require more privacy in winter, simply increase the amounts of holly and wild privet.

A mixed hedge such as this will not reach the heights of many conifer hedges, but this can be a bonus. If height is required, intersperse some hedgerow trees, which will contribute an additional tier of foliage towards the desired woodland edge effect (see page 106). This multiple canopy allows you to fit in more plants and create an interesting, rich and varied habitat that will go a little way towards helping to replace all those thousands of acres of woodland that are steadily being ripped out.

Plan a border that will flower very early and also very late (annuals are useful here) and include flowers with edible seed heads.

Planting

When planting a border, try to pack in as many plants as you can that will attract butterflies – the presence of some dazzling peacocks, holly blues and painted ladies will really bring your garden to life and you will be doing your bit to preserve the many species that are being driven to the edge of extinction as chemical spraying destroys their habitats.

Mauve and purple plants, such as buddleias, lilac, lavender, valerian and *Eupatorium purpureum*, hold a special attraction for butterflies, as do native and commonly naturalized plants, such as *Viburnum lantana* (wayfaring tree), *V. opulus* (guelder rose), *Ajuga reptans* (bugle), *Dipsacus fullonum* (teasel) and *Hesperis matronalis* (sweet rocket). For bees, plant *Cistus* spp. (rock roses), *Laurus nobilis* (bay), potentillas, spiraea and foxgloves.

This colourful border contains buddleia pink delight and *Eupatorium purpureum*, both of which attract butterflies.

Maintenance

If you do not wish to change the mixture of plants in your borders, try a more sympathetic maintenance regime. Instead of chopping all your herbaceous plants down in the autumn, leave the stems so that hollow stalks will provide a habitat for insects. When spring comes, cut the stalks down to allow the new growth to emerge and chop them up to form a mulch over the soil. Mulches reduce the amount of weeds able to germinate and keep the moisture in the ground through dry summers, providing a good habitat for insects. Avoid fine bark mulches, which are an excellent germinating medium for weeds and also absorb moisture so that in dry periods plant roots grow up towards the damp rather than forming a healthy deep root system.

Plant	Soil suitability		
Acer campestre (field maple)		Normal	Dry
Cornus sanguinea (common dogwood)	Wet	Normal	
Crataegus monogyna (common hawthorn)	Wet	Normal	
Euonymous europaeus (spindle)	Wet	Normal	Dry
Hippophae rhamnoides (sea buckthorn)	Wet	Normal	Dry
Ilex aquifolium (common holly)		Normal	Dry
Ligustrum vulgare (common privet)		Normal	Dry
Rhamnus catharticus (common buckthorn)		Normal	Dry
Rhamnus frangula (alder buckthorn)		Normal	Dry
Rosa canina (dog rose)		Normal	Dry
Viburnum lantana (wayfaring tree)		Normal	Dry
Viburnum opulus (guelder rose)	Wet	Normal	

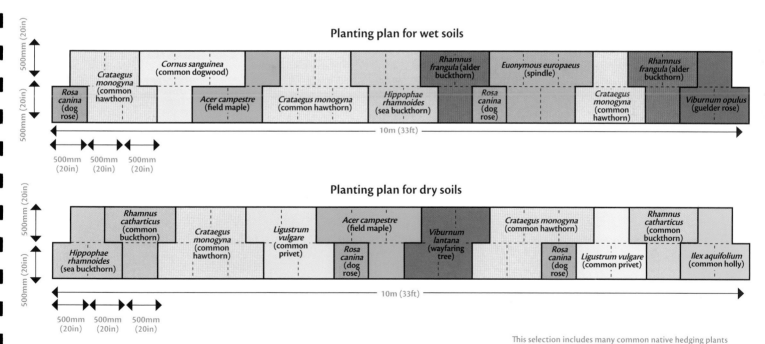

Planting plan for wet soils

Planting plan for dry soils

This selection includes many common native hedging plants that will tolerate the conditions indicated in the chart. For a really stout hedge plant a fairly high proportion of hawthorn and only use a sprinkling of dog rose for decoration.

PETS IN THE GARDEN

Most children yearn for a pet of some sort and indeed many families feel life's not complete without a furred or feathered companion or two. Pets can mean damaged borders and unsightly hutches and runs, but with a bit of forethought the pleasures will far outweigh the pain. The possibility of disease is also a concern for parents, but simple precautions can make it a remote one (see box).

Chickens are productive pets that are simple to look after. They become extremely tame and usually mix well with rabbits and guinea pigs.

Dogs

In terms of playmates for children, dogs cannot be beaten – they will usually join enthusiastically in any activity, particularly if it involves running, jumping and scrambling. For a keen gardener, though, the top priority is to teach dogs not to go on, or dig in, borders. This message can usually be got across in one afternoon's weeding spent with a new puppy. It may be ignored in moments of excitement but once they are past that first flush of puppyish exuberance (usually at about nine months) dogs will rarely step on borders again.

Cats

All a cat really asks from a garden is somewhere to sharpen its claws and a sunny spot in which to snooze. However, some clumps of *Nepeta* x *faassenii* (catmint) as a bonus will send most cats dizzy with delight. For a home-made version of the catnip mice that are sold in pet shops, dry some *Nepeta*, sew it into piece of cloth and tie a length of string to it. The children will enjoy dragging it around the garden to entice the cat into some action.

Rabbits

These come in a range of varieties from standard bunnies to lop-eared, plush-coated creatures that wouldn't look out of place on a soft toy counter. The simple solution to rabbit runs cluttering up the garden is to build one that you like looking at, such as the one in the project on pp. 112–113.

A small area in the corner of the garden with all the paraphernalia such as food bins and winter hutches screened from sight gives children some scope for organizing their 'pets' corner' in the way they want.

Chickens

Chickens are fascinating to watch as they scratch around and they have the added bonus of providing truly fresh eggs. Their only drawback is that they are partial to certain plants, particularly hostas and lettuces. The best plan is to confine them to a pen for most of the day during the growing season and allow them a freer run in the winter months, restricting them to the informal areas of the garden – an orchard provides an ideal setting.

A bird table like this allows you to hang food from it as well as placing it on the table. To prevent the build-up of disease, move the table annually.

Dogs are deservedly one of the most popular pets, and with discipline can easily be taught to stay away from borders and ornamental pools.

Disease	Prevention
Myxomatosis This disease affects rabbits only.	Inoculate pet rabbits against it to prevent infection from wild rabbits.
Toxocariasis Eggs of the roundworm *Toxocara* passed in faeces of infected dogs can contaminate children's hands. If eggs are swallowed there is a slight possibility of toxocariasis, which usually only causes slight flu-like symptoms. In rare cases vision may be impaired; total blindness is rarer still.	Worm puppies at two weeks old and at least four more times before they are six months old; train them to soil in a specific area and tell your children to avoid this patch of the garden. Worm adult dogs at least every six months. Freshly passed faeces are not a toxocariasis hazard as the eggs take two to three weeks to mature, so clean up all dog faeces regularly. Remind the children to wash their hands after playing with pets. If you inherit a garden from a dog-owner, bear in mind that *Toxocara* eggs can live for up to three years.
Toxoplasmosis Toxoplasmosis is caused by a tiny parasite, *Toxoplasma gondii*, found in most animals and birds, in garden soil and on fresh vegetables. Cats excrete *Toxoplasma* eggs in their faeces if they pick up an infection from wild birds, mice or raw meat. Toxoplasmosis is not usual dangerous to healthy adults or children, but if a woman catches it for the first time while she is pregnant the infection may damage the sight and brain of the foetus and/or cause epilepsy.	Pregnant women should wear gloves when gardening or handling cat litter/faeces and wash hands afterwards. Cover sand pits to prevent cats using them.

PROJECT: A RABBIT HUTCH OR RUN

This attractive run is designed for rabbits and guinea pigs, though it could comfortably be used for a couple of bantams or small chickens, in which case a nesting box and perch should be added in the covered part, making sure it gives them enough headroom.

You will need

- One sheet of 19mm (¾in) WBP (exterior grade) plywood, 1220 x 2440mm (48 x 96in), to form four arches, three roof braces, and two doors and adjacent uprights
- Two sheets of 6mm (¼in) WBP plywood, 1220 x 2440mm (48 x 96in), to form the floor and cladding strips (and beam compass)
- Six lengths of hardwood dowelling 690mm x 19mm (27⅛ x ¾in) diameter
- Two horizontal base beams 25 x 50 x 2026mm (1 x 2 x 79¾in), hardwood or tanalized softwood
- Four arch braces 25 x 50 x 820mm (1 x 2 x 32¼in) hardwood or tanalized softwood
- Chicken netting 8m (26ft 3in) x 900mm (36in) wide
- One turn button
- One door bolt, 63mm (2½in) long
- Weatherproof woodworking adhesive
- 25mm (1in) x 1.8mm (¹⁄₁₆in) galvanized wire nails
- 15mm (⅝in) x 1.6mm (¹⁄₁₆in) galvanized staples
- 38mm (1½in) x No. 8 plated woodscrews
- Non-toxic wood stain (dark brown)

Tools
- Jigsaw • Plane • Hammer
- Drill and wood bits
- Tenon saw • Screwdriver
- Wire cutters or tin snips
- Panel saw • Try square

Marking out the frame

1 Make a template for the central roof brace by taping a piece of card the size of the surrounding rectangle across one end of a plywood sheet (see diagram opposite). Make a beam compass from a strip of 6mm (¼in) plywood, with a nail through one end and holes for a pencil at radii of 2100 and 2025mm (82⅝ and 79⅝in) from it. Use this to mark the curves.

2 Mark out the arches on the plywood, following the cutting plan opposite. Mark the centre line of each arch, both for marking the curves and to help in positioning the roof braces later. Cut the beam compass down for the arch radii of 410mm and 360mm (16⅛ and 14⅛in). The partition arch is solid except for the access hole, which must be large enough to let through the future occupant. Position it to one side (at least

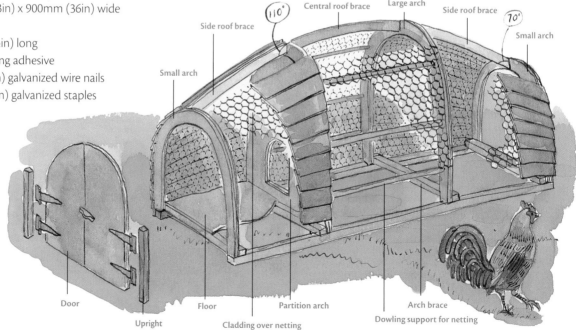

Side roof brace
Central roof brace
Large arch
Side roof brace
Small arch
Small arch
Door
Upright
Floor
Cladding over netting
Partition arch
Arch brace
Dowling support for netting

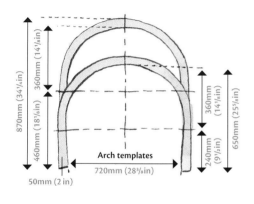

Arch templates

870mm (34¹/₄in)
360mm (14¹/₄in)
460mm (18¹/₂in)
50mm (2 in)
720mm (28³/₈in)
360mm (14¹/₄in)
240mm (9¹/₂in)
650mm (25⁵/₈in)

75mm/3in from the edge) to leave a relatively draught-proof area on the other side.

3 Mark out the rectangles for the roof braces and mark the 70° angled ends on the side braces, either using a protractor or by measuring in from the ends of the rectangle. Use the template to mark on the curves; those on the side braces are offset within the rectangles. The side braces are mirror images of each other, so make them identical and turn one end over end when fitting it.

Central roof brace template

690mm (27¹/₈in)   38mm (1¹/₂in)
150mm (4⁷/₈in)

Side roof brace template

110°   70°
38mm (1¹/₂in)   708mm (27⁷/₈in)
150mm (4⁷/₈in)

4 Cut out the marked components close to the lines to leave undamaged plywood for the doors and their supports. Smooth all edges with medium glasspaper.

Assembling the frame

5 Glue and screw the four arch braces to one face of each arch, with the 50mm (2in) face against the plywood. Lay the two horizontal base beams flat on the ground, parallel to each other, and with the inner edges 720mm (28³/₈in) apart.

6 Set up the arches squarely on the base beams, with the flat face of the small arches flush with the ends of the beams, and the large arches spaced 630mm (24³/₄in) away from them so that their braces face away from the centre. (There should be 690mm/27¹/₈in between the large arches.) Glue and screw them to the beams.

7 Position the central roof brace with its thickness centred on the marked centre line of the two large arches and the outer curve flush with their top edges. Glue and screw it in place with two screws into each end. Offset the side roof braces from the central one sufficiently to allow the screws to be inserted, then fix them in the same way.

8 Cut out the hutch floor 630 x 820mm (24³/₄ x 32¹/₄in) from 6mm (¹/₄in) plywood. Nail it to the arch braces in the partition arch section.

9 To maintain the shape of the netting in the middle section, glue and screw the dowelling at equal distances to span the gap between the large arches.

Finishing the hutch

10 The two doors overlap the end arch by 25mm (1in). Cut them to a height of 625mm (24¹/₂in) with a top radius of 385mm

(15¹/₈in). Cut the two uprights, 25 x 240mm (1 x 9¹/₂in), to take the vertical hinge flaps, and glue and screw them to the small arch, flush with the outer and bottom edges. Screw the hinges to the doors and fix them to the uprights with one screw per hinge, to check for fit. Plane down the long edges as necessary, then refix.

11 Screw the turn button 12mm (¹/₂in) in from the edge of one door and screw the bolt to the inside of the same door so that it just clears the floor in the raised position. Screw a small plywood block to the face of the arch brace and drill a hole in it to take the bolt.

12 Apply two coats of preservative wood stain to all assembled components first; you could also paint one face of the 6mm (¹/₄in) plywood to give added protection.

13 Cut chicken netting to cover the top and one end. Pleat the netting over the end sections, so that it lies flat, and fix it to all edges of the frame with galvanized staples.

14 Cut 90 x 800mm (3¹/₂ x 31¹/₂in) strips of 6mm (¹/₄in) plywood, along the length of the sheets, for cladding the two end sections. Starting at the bottom, nail the strips to the arches; trim all ends flush, except round the doors where they should project by 10mm (³/₈in). Overlap each previous strip by 30mm (1¹/₄in) at the outer end and 10mm (³/₈in) at the inner end. Cover the gap at the top with a trapezium of plywood, 740mm (29¹/₈in) long, with ends 140 and 180mm (5¹/₂ and 7in) wide (or to fit), nailed to the arches and the side roof braces.

15 Paint the hutch with two coats of non-toxic preservative wood stain, allowing the odour to wear off completely before using the run.

THE PLANTING SCHEME

Planting to please every member of the family requires careful selection and planning if the garden is to fulfil the many functions demanded of it. Some areas may call for tough plants that will survive ball games, den-making and general hurly-burly relatively unscathed, while others will need to be sufficiently interesting and attractive to satisfy the horticulturally minded.

PLANTING DESIGNS

Gardeners frequently have problems with the arrangement of the plants in their borders. They are often dissatisfied with the overall result but do not know how to rectify it. Undoubtedly it is a complex business, for not only must plants thrive in the conditions that prevail in your garden, but they must also perform as part of an orchestrated sequence so that the whole border looks good through the changing seasons.

Common reasons for borders falling short of the mark is that they look spotty, incohesive and lack a definite style. To prevent this happening in your garden borders, concentrate on the overall impression and character you want to create in each different section of the garden before you start to think about which particular plants to grow. For example, decide whether you want a pastel-coloured cottage garden feel, a bold tropical effect or a colour-led theme and plant accordingly.

A planting plan

Having established the style of planting you are aiming for, set about producing a plan. In the illustrations opposite you can see three different ways to plan a border. Plants must be carefully placed in a border even if the look you wish to achieve is wild and natural. In the designs opposite, a strong pattern is provided by a low clipped hedge, punctuated with repeated groups of shrubs.

When you plant a new border, ensure that it looks reasonably full as soon as possible. Propagate or purchase several of each species and do not be afraid to plant them close together. The only possible downside is that in periods of drought the competition for moisture is greater, but you can water well to compensate. Otherwise, as a temporary measure, fill the gaps with annuals or quick-to-establish fillers that are easy to propagate yourself, such as *Alchemilla mollis* (lady's mantle), *Nepeta* (catmint) and *Senecio* Dunedin Hybrid 'Sunshine'. Using plants that self-seed will also quickly give the garden a look of maturity and provide exciting new developments from year to year. In due course you may pull them out once the more choice players come into their own.

Finally, planting design is a challenge, given the many variables to consider. However, do not despair. While you might not get it right all the time, that is half the fun of gardening – trying different types of plants in different places to create different effects. Although the structure of the garden and choice of hard landscaping materials are important, it is the plants that add the dramatic, dynamic element to a garden, constantly changing as they grow and develop through the seasons and years. Regular reappraisal of your garden plantings will allow you to try new and exciting combinations in areas that seem to be flagging or lacking in interest.

The natural feel of this garden is achieved through skilful planting with a wonderful use of colour.

This garden exudes an exciting subtropical air. Bold-foliaged plants, such as the 'hardy' banana *Musa basjoo*, will survive out-of-doors, all year round in temperate zones with the protection of hessian covering during cold snaps.

KEY

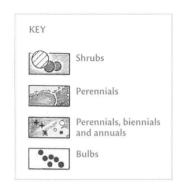

Shrubs

Perennials

Perennials, biennials and annuals

Bulbs

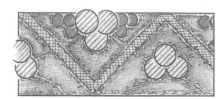

Here, the strong co-ordinating element is the low box hedge; this divides the bed into triangles that are filled with repeat groupings of shrubs and herbaceous plants. The bed could look smart and neatly trimmed, or informal, with laxer growing plants softening the lines of the hedges. Topiary could be used to punctuate the planting groups, particularly in winter.

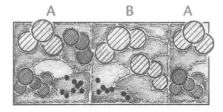

This design shows a more traditional approach. Here a longer stretch of planting has been broken up and planted alternately with two different groups of plants (A and B). This gives a long border a definite unity. More than two groups could be repeated or, in a shorter border, just repeat certain elements, such as a group of shrubs and two distinctive groups of herbaceous plants.

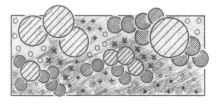

This design shows a much more random approach, ideal for a wilder part of the garden. Groups of larger plants have been dotted through areas of lower plants. Some of these are accent plants, with eye-catching foliage or contrasting flowers. The result is a lush jungle effect; to maintain cohesion, repeat groups of plants and use self-seeding varieties that will appear informally, filling any unplanted spaces.

PROTECTING THE GARDEN

The joy of gardening for me and many adults is focused mainly around plants, and the damage caused to them by stray balls, children's feet and pet dogs can be heartbreaking. However, an alternative to banishing children from these treasured areas is to plant up certain parts of the garden with child-friendly plants or to protect prized specimens with barrier planting.

Tough plants for play

Patches of tough plants will become the children's domain in which they can trample undergrowth, dig holes, whittle stems, pick flowers and make dens to their hearts' content. In the foreground of these tough plant beds, establish drifts of prolific self-seeders such as foxgloves, mullein or valerian.

Shrub willows
Several varieties have striking coloured stems that appeal to children. They establish quickly, creating an ideal den-making environment, and also grow back rapidly after being damaged. It is the young shoots that display the brightest coloration, so cut the old stems back to about 150mm (6in) every other year in late spring after the winter display. The new shoots will emerge rapidly.

Bamboo jungles
A large thicket of the more vigorous bamboo creates an instant mini-jungle and as a result holds endless possibilities for children (but beware, they do make excellent spears). The most suitable varieties are those with a tendency towards thuggish behaviour, such as *Pseudosasa japonica*. This is an adaptable beast, forming canes up to 4.5m (15ft) high, or sometimes even 6m (20ft). It bears lush masses of glossy green leaves up to 300mm (12in) long.

Quick-recovery plants
Tree mallows grow easily from cuttings at phenomenal speeds and flower non-stop throughout the spring and summer months given a suitable, sunny site. *Cornus* (dogwood), *Corylus avenana* (native hazel), *Ligustrum* (privet) and *Prunus laurocerasus* (common laurel) are all easy to establish and recover quickly after damage. For smaller gardens, *Hypericum* 'Hidcote' is useful and is ideal for making tunnels in! All the hebes are renowned for their powers of recovery, though the taller ones such as *H.* 'Midsummer Beauty' and *H. brachysiphon* give more scope for creating secret worlds.

Ground cover
The play area will look more attractive if the soil is covered. In summer this will be taken care of by the self-seeding plants, but the simplest method to maintain the cover through winter is a good layer of coarse-grade bark. Alternatively, a vigorous ground-cover plant (see Tough Plant Directory) will increase the level of interest.

Barrier plants

The best way to achieve flourishing borders is to site the more delicate plants away from the main zone of robust activity. If your garden is too small for this, then site

them behind a protective layer of toughies. Whatever you plant in a vulnerable position, allow it to establish itself before you let the children loose. A temporary fence of sticks and string, coupled with much discipline, may be necessary until the plants get going.

Formal barrier
In my garden, the choice borders have a low hedge of box, which clearly demarcates the front edge of the border and forms the start of a 'no-go zone'. I chose *Buxus sempervirens*, which quickly forms a thick, robust hedge. Box edging may also follow a strong, scalloped line or a gentle curve.

Informal edging
For a slightly more relaxed look, *Hebe anomala* is excellent and grows quickly to form a good hedge; it also regenerates well if knocked about a bit. The larger potentillas work well, although the plants behind them must be at least 1m (3ft) high, otherwise they will be hidden away.

Tougher plants
If you do not want to define borders with a hedge, then simply fill the more vulnerable front areas in the beds with plants from the Barrier Plant Directory. Most of these are fairly common and their popularity stems from the fact that they are easy to grow and shoot back quickly after being trampled on.

Tough plant directory

Shrubs and trees

Bamboo
The taller bamboos (*Pseudosasa japonica* and *Fargesia spathacea*) provide clumps and thickets for dens. Most are hardy but dislike high winds and drought.

Buddleia (butterfly bush)
Rapidly growing plants that bloom quickly with brightly coloured spires and attract butterflies.

Cornus (dogwood)
Establish fast; in winter the young stems of several varieties are a bright colour. *Cornus alba* 'Elegantissima' is less vigorous for small spaces.

Cortaderia (pampas grass)
This looks at its best in groups of 3–5; *C. selloana* 'Sunningdale Silver' grows up to 3–4m (10–13ft) high, with silver plumes.

Corylus avellana (native hazel)
A small hazel thicket provides a play environment and a supply of sticks for supporting peas and making archways.

Eleaegnus x ebbingei
This is a fast, tough evergreen with a dense habit that responds well to cutting back.

Hypericum
Recover well. *H.* 'Hidcote' has a compact habit, giving dense wood for forming tunnels. Large, saucer-shaped yellow flowers over a long period.

Kerria
Tall, graceful shrubs with green stems, which spread readily by suckers. *K. japonica* 'Pleniflora' has double, rich yellow flowers and arching branches.

Lavatera thuringiaca (mallow)
Fast-growing elegant shrubs with greyish, downy stems and leaves; flowers produced from summer to late autumn.

Ligustrum (privet)
These recover well. *Ligustrum vulgare* (native privet) is partially evergreen and more open than *Ligustrum ovalifolium*.

Prunus laurocerasus (common laurel)
This large shrub can grow into a small tree although it responds well to cutting back. It forms a fast-growing evergreen screen.

Salix (willow)
Open shrubs that recover well. To maintain the bright stem colour, cut back hard each second year.

Sambucus (elder)
Quick to establish and tolerant. Avoid the common elder as it is rather coarse in appearance and seeds prolifically. Try *S. nigra* 'Aurea' (golden elder) or *S. nigra* 'Purpurea' (purple-leaved elder).

Symphoricarpus
These are quite hardy and are suited to dry shade among trees. *S. albus* (snowberry) forms dense clumps, ideal for secret dens.

Viburnum lantana (wayfaring tree)
A native hedgerow plant that recovers well from damage; creamy white flowers in late spring to early summer.

Ground-cover plants

Hedera (ivy)
Many of the ivies form good dense ground cover, and are economical and quick to establish, such as *H. hibernica* (Irish ivy).

Vinca major (periwinkle)
This forms attractive swathes of ground cover and has bright blue flowers. Can become invasive.

Euonymus
Come in different tones of green, gold, white and cream. They vary in height and vigour.

Plants from the Tough Plant Directory (see above) could be used in addition to the ones below.

Barrier plant directory

Shrubs

Buxus sempervirens (box)
A large species that can also be used as a low hedge. It will need clipping twice a year, but it establishes much faster and forms a more robust barrier than the commonly used *B.* 'Suffruticosa'.

Cotoneaster varieties
Come in all shapes and sizes from ground-hugging to small trees; some are evergreen.

Erica (heaths and heathers)
Includes well-foliaged 'cushions' that will soon re-grow after misuse.

Hebe varieties
Grow back well following damage, provided that they are young, healthy specimens.

Mahonia aquifolium
A useful, evergreen plant that spreads by suckers. It tolerates poor soils and has fragrant yellow flowers in spring.

Potentilla varieties
Are excellent plants that can be used for low-growing hedges. They flower for long periods and tolerate poor soils.

Pyracantha 'Soleil d'Or'
A useful, spreading evergreen with yellow berries.

Senecio Dunedin Hybrid 'Sunshine'
An invaluable evergrey shrub, which is quick to establish and shoots back well after damage.

Stephanandra incisa 'Crispa'
A very reliable, deciduous ground-cover plant.

Weigela varieties
Have profuse flowers in midsummer.

Herbaceous plants

Alchemilla mollis (lady's mantle)
Has attractive leaves and green-yellow flowers in midsummer.

Ballota pseudodictamnus
A white, woolly subshrub or perennial, with round, felted leaves.

Bergenia varieties
Form a useful, bold-leaved, evergreen ground cover, and are fairly tough.

Euphorbia robbiae (spurge)
An attractive evergreen with showy, lime-green bracts. It can be invasive and grows to 600mm (2ft) high.

Geranium varieties
All the vigorous herbaceous geraniums are excellent, tough, colourful ground-cover plants.

Lamium (deadnettle)
The less invasive *L. maculatum* 'Beacon Silver' and *L m.* 'Chequers' are quick-spreading, carpeting plants.

Nepeta (catmint)
Has scented grey foliage and lavender-blue flowers all summer.

Polygonum (knotgrass)
Includes some good, tough carpeters.

Stachys byzantina (lamb's ears)
A familiar plant, loved by children for its furry, grey leaves.

SIMPLE PLANTS FOR CHILDREN TO GROW

The unfurling of new leaves and the blossoming of flowers can seem magical to a child, and the beauty of this is that it is so attainable; many plants can be grown in a small space on a balcony, or even a windowsill. You will find that children will pick, wash and eat their own vegetables with gusto.

Choosing plants

Younger children with a shorter concentration span should grow plants that will do something notable sooner rather than later. Avoid seeds that are prone to rot, have poor germination or need lots of heat – go for a safe bet initially and purchase small bedding or vegetable plants (though many vegetable seeds are easy to grow). Pelleted seed is much easier for small children to handle and so can be sown more precisely. See also pp. 122-123 for a list of Children's Favourites.

Vegetables
• Courgettes are good value, with large yellow flowers that are slowly pushed off by the rapidly growing vegetables.
• Onions or shallots from sets are very easy.
• Lettuce, be it red or green, germinates very fast and is soon ready to eat.
• Peas and beans have large seeds and are quick to respond when sown.

Flowers
• Sweet peas are easy to grow and have large seeds for easy planting.
• Pansies have a smaller seed, but are still manageable. Broadcast outside in the soil in early spring.
• Cornflowers sown in early spring will come up within a week, and can be broadcast in a mix with native poppies.
• Nigella, or love-in-a-mist, grows fast, has a reasonable-sized seed and is exquisite in flower.
• *Papaver nudicaule* (Iceland poppies) come in a colourful range of apricot, orange, yellow and scarlet and look dramatic broadcast in patches in the border.
• Lupins are a striking perennial to grow; the hard seed case can be rubbed between two pieces of fine sandpaper to hasten germination.
• *Tropaeolum* (nasturtium), *Consolida* (larkspur), *Salvia*, *Helianthus* (sunflower), *Lavatera trimestris* (mallow) and *Calendula* (marigold) are all colourful, quick and easy too.

Children enjoy doing things with their plants – admittedly not always the type of things one would expect. Plants such as pumpkins, runner beans, squashes and trailing nasturtiums are ideal, as they can fiddle with the stems and encourage them to climb up a homemade wigwam or fence.

Brightly coloured vegetables, such as the purple beetroot 'Bull's Blood', ornamental cabbages and red cut-and-come-again lettuce can be interspersed with some annual flowers to form growing letters, numbers, pictures and patterns.

A selection of tree seedlings in pots decorate this spare corner, and the children have created a temporary garden with them.

Tree seeds

Sowing seed is a surprisingly rapid way of establishing trees, though some seeds are slow to germinate – ash being one example. Oak seeds, conversely, may have already sent out roots before you have collected them. Other trees that are easy to grow are horse chestnut, beech, walnut, hazel, silver birch and alder.

In autumn, sow the freshly collected seeds individually at the same depth as their size in deep pots with about 25mm (1in) of free-draining material in the base and moist compost to just below the top. Your two main problems will probably be mice and rot, so cover your pots with a fine wire mesh and do not overwater, though the compost should be kept moist. When the weather warms up in spring, the seeds should start to sprout. As soon as the root system has a good hold, move the seedlings to their final position and water them well for the first month or so. If they are not ready to move out until summer, leave them until the autumn; any that do not germinate the first year can be left in situ for another year. Do not allow weeds or grass to compete with them for several years.

Encourage young gardeners by providing easy-to-grow plants that perform quickly, such as bedding plants on the point of flowering.

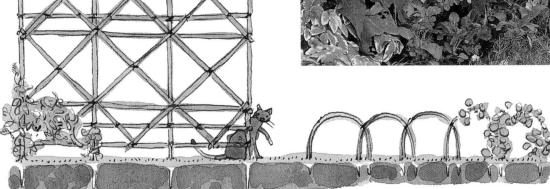

Hazel fences are ideal boundaries around a child's plot. The hurdle fence (right) is a useful and attractive way to demarcate areas or bend the wood when it is pliable to form small tunnels, ideal for training climbers.

CHILDREN'S FAVOURITES

There are some plants that will keep younger children happy for hours, though they are not always ones the adults want to have around – such as dandelions, whose clocks can be blown around the garden to set seed in yet more places, and daisies, which can be woven into chains. Older children will probably still deign to play with these from time to time, but they will also enjoy plants they can actually do something with. 'Step-over' apples, which can be trained to form an edging around a plot as well as supplying fruit, give very good value.

Strawberry plants in a strawberry pot are colourful and easy, and it is fun to help increase the quantity of fruit set by tickling the flowers with a small paintbrush.

If you can, allocate your children a small area of garden that is free from invasive weeds and has good, easy-to-work soil with a sunny aspect, and encourage them to grow some of the more child-friendly plants to kindle their gardening instincts. A diverse range of plants, varying the mix from year to year, will broaden their horizons, but until they are confident gardeners it is best to stick with easy-to-grow species.

Topiary

The addition of some topiary to a garden can add a touch of grandeur, formality or fun, transforming even an ordinary garden into one that seems quite special. The job of clipping, shaping and growing it is soothing and quite absorbing, and if you get it wrong you can correct it next time round.

Many plants can be used but the most common are *Laurus nobilis* (bay), *Fagus sylvatica* (beech), *Buxus sempervirens* (box), *Juniperus communis* (juniper), *Crataegus monogyna* (hawthorn), *Ilex aquifolium* (holly), *Carpinus betulus* (hornbeam), *Ligustrum ovalifolium* (privet) and *Taxus baccata* (yew).

When you start your topiary, try to go with the natural form of the plant as far as possible. You will find that simple geometric shapes are the easiest to start with; you can either do these by eye or use strings as a guide. If you go for a more complex shape you may need supports of canes and wire, but take care not to constrict the stems too much.

This fine specimen bird was assembled, planted, trained and trimmed up all in one growing season. He will, however, require regular tender loving care to keep him in such fine fettle.

Children will love creating a cat like this, and with a bit of help from an adult, it is quite feasible.

Plants of interest to children

Trees

Betula pendula 'Youngii' (weeping birch)
These small weeping birches quickly form small dens for younger children.

Fraxinus excelsior 'Pendula' (weeping ash)
A more unusual weeping tree that will form a pleasing den.

Malus domestica 'Ballerina' (orchard apple)
These trees grow on one vertical stem requiring little space and no pruning or stakes, crop heavily and quickly and can be grown in tubs.

Malus domestica Step-over apples (orchard apple)
These trees are trained to form a low 'step over' fence, so make an ideal productive fence around a child's (or adult's) plot.

Malus 'Golden Hornet' (crab apple)
A crab apple on the dwarfing rootstock M27 will form a tree no more than 1.5m (5ft) high, an ideal size for a child's tiny garden. It produces white flowers and bright yellow fruits.

Prunus spp. (sweet cherry)
These are good trees for small tree houses, with the bonus of blossom and cherries.

Shrubs, grasses, herbaceous and aquatic plants

Bamboos
The larger bamboos produce long canes that are useful for constructing dens, temporary fences and archways. The plants themselves can make ideal dens.

Buddleia spp. (butterfly bush)
This shrub is often covered in butterflies. It will grow in poor, dry soils, so is a good plant for a container.

Corylus avellana (cobnut)
As well as producing long yellow catkins, this shrub will provide wonderful wands for making archways, dens, fences and so on, with edible nuts as a further bonus. Try also *C. a.* 'Contorta', which has curious twisted branches.

Digitalis purpurea (foxglove)
This easy, pretty plant has bold purple-spotted flowers that bumble bees favour. All parts of the plant are poisonous and the foliage can sometimes cause a skin reaction, but provided children are supervised and warned of the dangers it can be grown.

Salix caprea (pussy willow)
This native willow will quickly grow to about 3m (9ft) tall and can be coppiced. The furry silver catkins fascinate children. A small group of these could form the basis of a tough den.

Annuals, soft fruit and vegetables

Antirrhinum majus (snapdragon)
Children like to pinch the blossoms and make the 'dragon mouth' open and close.

Fragaria x ananassa (strawberry)
Strawberry planters that house several plants per pot are an interesting way to grow them.

Cucurbita maxima (pumpkin)
Children can have great fun training these up stout canes and then making lanterns out of the massive mature fruits.

Cucurbita pepo (ornamental gourd)
These are purely ornamental, but they are attractive and fun to grow.

Helichrysum bracteatum (everlasting flowers)
The flowers of this plant are excellent for drying. When fresh they have a crisp texture, and come in bold colours.

Helianthus annuus (common sunflower)
This rapid-growing giant-sized plant with magnificent brightly coloured flowers is a long-established favourite with children.

Impatiens walleriana (busy Lizzie)
A prolific flowerer that can be brought into the house in the winter as a pot plant, and is easy to increase by means of cuttings.

Mimosa pudica (sensitive plant)
Easily grown from seed, this plant has ferny foliage that folds together when touched. Grow as an annual in the garden or as a pot plant.

Physalis franchetii (Chinese lantern)
This plant has bright orange papery lanterns enclosing a cherrylike berry, which is attractive in winter arrangements.

Physalis edulis (Cape gooseberry)
This has 'magic lanterns' enclosing the most delicious orange fruits; these can be eaten raw, dipped in white chocolate or made into jam. A must for children.

Other plants

Cacti
Children often have a cactus as their first plant. Many of these spiny plants take little looking after and occasionally produce stunning flowers.

Dionaea muscipula (Venus flytrap)
This carnivorous plant is satisfyingly gruesome to watch as the traps (which become red in sunlight) catch a fly and slowly absorb it.

Pleiospilos bolusii (living rock)
These small succulents grow in clumps exactly resembling stones and are an unusual plant for a child to grow indoors. They produce golden-yellow flowers in early autumn.

COMMON POISONOUS PLANTS

Plants are responsible for only a small proportion of accidents around the home, and these are rarely serious. However, it does pay to make it clear to children that they should not sample any plants except those that you have confirmed to be edible.

Apart from the list here of common toxic plants, there are many others that although not deadly, can provoke severe reactions if certain parts are eaten. These include many widely grown garden plants such as anemone, aquilegia, arum, bryony, *Buxus* (box), *Hedera* (ivy), hellebore, juniper, kalmia, *Ligustrum* (privet), lobelia, lupin, clematis, *Convallaria majalis* (lily of the valley), daffodil, *Robinia pseudocacia* (false acacia), *Sambucus* (elder), foxglove, tomatoes, potatoes, *Rheum* (rhubarb), *Symphytum* (comfrey) and wisteria, to name a few. To exclude all these from your garden would be impractical: it is unlikely that a child would eat quantities of elder foliage, for example.

Even in the case of the plants in the Poisonous Plant Directory, I include *Taxus* (yew) and *Aconitum* (monkshood) in my garden. When children are too young to comprehend but old enough to be mobile – usually a short period – they are closely watched. Older children can understand that they should treat the plant with respect.

The majority of plants have not been tested for toxicity, so do not assume that any plants not described as toxic are necessarily harmless. Bear in mind that some plants can cause other injuries – for instance, the tips of yucca leaves are often at the right height for a young child's eye, and rough-edged leaves, rose thorns and so on can also inflict a wound. Make sure that tetanus vaccinations are kept up to date.

If any of the plants described in the list opposite as severely toxic are eaten, you should seek urgent medical help from your doctor or an accident and emergency department. Take a sample of the plant with you, do not panic and do not make the patient sick.

Treat *Heracleum mantegazzianum* (giant hogweed) with respect as it is severely toxic when eaten.

Poisonous plant directory

Aconitum spp. (monkshood)
All parts of the plant are severely toxic, especially the roots. The chemicals in the foliage cause skin irritation.

Aethusa cynapium (fool's parsley)
This common weed could be mistaken for parsley by a child. Its degree of toxicity is uncertain.

Atropa belladonna (deadly nightshade)
All parts of this native perennial are severely toxic, and the black berries may well be tempting to children.

Conium maculatum (hemlock)
All parts of this tall white flowering weed are severely toxic. The plant can also cause allergic skin reactions.

Datura spp. (angels' trumpets)
All parts of these plants are severely toxic.

Euphorbia spp. (spurge)
These widely grown plants are toxic if eaten, though not severely so. The more common problem is an allergic skin reaction that may occur in some individuals. Blisters, redness and itching may occur up to six days after contact.

Gloriosa superba (glory lily)
All parts of this stunning flowered deciduous climber are severely toxic if eaten, and the tubers will cause a skin reaction similar to a mild chemical burn, though this is unlikely to be serious or long-lasting.

Heracleum mantegazzianum (giant hogweed)
If eaten this spectacular plant is severely toxic. The more common complaint is that when the sap comes in contact with the skin in strong sunlight it sensitizes it, causing bad sunburn, itching and burning followed by dramatic blisters. The damage to the skin may last for six months or more; the other effects wear off in a few weeks.

Hyoscyamus niger (henbane)
This unpleasant smelling annual/biennial weed has dull creamy yellow, bell-shaped flowers with purple veins. It is common on bare and disturbed ground, particularly near the sea. All parts of the plant are severely toxic and can also cause skin irritation.

Ipomoea spp. (morning glory)
The seeds of these plants are severely toxic.

Laburnum spp.
All parts of these trees are severely toxic, especially the seeds, which resemble peas in a pod.

Colchicum spp.
All parts of these spring- and autumn-flowering plants are severely toxic if eaten and may also cause a skin reaction.

Daphne spp.
All parts of all these popular evergreen and deciduous shrubs are severely toxic if eaten, especially the seeds. The sap may cause a skin reaction similar to a mild chemical burn, although this is unlikely to be serious or long-lasting.

Nerium oleander (oleander)
All parts of these evergreen shrubs are severely toxic if eaten. In addition, some people may have an allergic skin reaction to the foliage, though this is unusual.

Nicotiana spp. (tobacco plant)
These attractive plants are severely toxic if any part of them is eaten. They may be a hazard to animals.

Ricinus communis (castor-oil plant)
All parts of this bold-foliaged plant are severely toxic, especially the seed. Contact with the foliage can also cause an allergic reaction in some people, resulting in blistering, redness and itching.

Ruta spp. (rue)
All parts of this plant are toxic if eaten, though not life-threateningly so. The foliage can irritate the skin and make it excessively sensitive to sunlight, causing severe sunburn often with itching and blistering. The itching usually disappears within a week or two, but the skin may be marked for six months or even more. Avoid coming into contact with this plant in strong sun.

Taxus spp. (yew)
All parts of this plant are severely toxic if eaten, though children will be most attracted by the berries. As it is often used for hedges, animals are more at risk.

Veratrum spp.
All parts of these shade-loving perennials are severely toxic if eaten. It is thought that the foliage may cause a skin reaction.

INDEX

Note: page numbers in **bold** refer to photographs and diagrams

LIST OF SUPPLIERS AND USEFUL ADDRESSES

Garden design

Werner de Bock, Landplan Associates, Barnwell All Saints, Peterborough, Cambs PE8 SPW.
Tel. 01832 272969
www.landplan-associates.co.uk

Peter Farrell, 49 Main Street, Woodnewton, Peterborough, Cambs PE8 5EB.
Tel. 01780 470066

Honor Gibbs, Consultant Landscape Architect, 89 Bicester Road, Long Crendon, Aylesbury, Bucks HP18 9EF.
Tel. 01844 208418

Bunny Guinness, Sibberton Lodge, Thornhaugh, Wansford, Cambs PE8 6NH.
Tel. 01780 782518
www.bunnyguinness.com

Play equipment

Hartland Limited, Unit 4, Manor Farm, Kingston Lisle, Wantage, Oxon OX12 9QL.
Tel. 01367 820005

Timber climbing frame (pp. 44–5)
New England Gardens Ltd, 22 Middle Street, Ashcott, Somerset TA7 9QB.
Tel. 01278 723400

TP Activity Toys available from stockists nationwide.
www.tptoys.com

Garden games
John Jaques and Sons Ltd, from stockists nationwide.
www.jaques.co.uk

Geotextile membrane e.g. 'Terram' manufactured by Terram Ltd and widely available from builder merchants.

Safety surfaces
Playbark available from Melcourt, Boldridge Brake, Long Newton, Tetbury, Glos GL8 8RT.
Tel. 01666 502711
www.melcourt.co.uk

Safety swing seats
Available from Wicksteed Leisure

Ltd, Digby Street, Kettering, Northants NN16 8YJ.
Tel. 01536 517028
www.wicksteed.co.uk

Features

Paddling pool fittings available from irrigation specialists Hortech Systems Ltd, Hall Gate, Holbeach, Spalding, Lincs PE12 7LG.
Tel. 01406 426513
www.hortechsystems.co.uk

Small paving units
Blanc de Bierges, Eastrea Road, Whittlesey, Peterborough, Cambs PE7 2AG.
Tel. 01733 202566
www.blancdebierges.com

Bound gravel
Imag Ltd, 5–7 Mill Street, Congleton, Cheshire CW12 1AB.
Tel. 01260 278810
www.imag.co.uk

Topiary frames
Capital Garden Products, Gibbs Reed Barn, Ticehurst, East Sussex

TN5 7HE.
Tel. 01580 201092
www.capital-garden.com

The Wadham Trading Company, Digbeth Street, Stow on the Wold, Glos GL54 1BN.
Tel. 01451 830308
www.wadhamtrading.co.uk

Buildings and furniture

Pavilion (p.78) from Andrew Crace Designs, Bourne Lane, Much Hadham, Herts SG10 6ER.
Tel. 01279 842685
www.andrewcrace.com

Nicholas Hodges Furniture, The Old Workshops, Church Walk, Wroxton, Banbury, Oxon OX11 6QF.
Tel. 01295 730362
www.hodgesfurniture.co.uk

Pets

Information available from: The Pet Health Council, 1 Bedford Avenue, London WC1B 3AU.
Tel. 020 7255 5408
www.pethealthcouncil.co.uk

ACKNOWLEDGMENTS

Firstly, I would like to thank my own family, my husband, Kevin, and my children, Unity and Freddie for all their invaluable help and inspiration, without which this book would never have materialized. I would also like to thank Anna Mumford of David & Charles for her help and support in making this book possible; the Art Editor, Lisa Tai, for her creativity, perserverance and unstinting hard work; Mike Trier for his input on the construction details; Juliette Wade for the superb photography and Kevin Hart for his excellent illustrations. Grateful thanks are also due to Stefan Wrobel for his imaginative contributions and much hard work in producing several of the plans and drawings. For the technical aspects, I would like to thank Rob Davies, Chief Engineer at Wicksteed Leisure Ltd for his advice on general construction details for play equipment and Anthony Blaine, John Simms and Peter Farrell for their advice on several of the construction details. Thanks are also due to all those in the horticultural industry I have contacted while writing this book who have, without exception, been extremely generous with their time and knowledge. I would particularly like to mention Margaret and Martyn Handley of Dingle Plants and Gardens, Pilsgate, Stamford for their generosity in providing a wide variety of wonderful plants.

I am indebted to the children who appeared in the photographs, especially William Clayton, Rory and Esme Farrell, Victoria Fox, Unity and Freddie Guinness, Andrew and David Mobbs, Alison Rea, the Sands children, Preeya and Arun Takhar and Thomas and Sarah Williams.

Finally, I am grateful to the following people for allowing us to photograph their gardens: Mr and Mrs J. Arlsford, David and Pat Ausbn, Chris and Jill Barnes, Peter and Ann Barnet, Mrs Susan Brooke, Mr and Mrs J. Conant, Chris and Janet Cottam, Graham and Heather Coulter, Mr and Mrs S. Dale, Werner and Jan de Bock, John and Anne Denning, Mr and Mrs Darby Dennis, Mrs Jane Dyer, Mr R. Edwards, Peter and Suzy Farrell, Mrs Helen Fickling, Prince and Princess Galitzine, Dr and Mrs Garton, Will Giles, Lady Gibberd, Barry and Honor Gibbs, Mrs Phillipa Gordon, Mrs Julia Greene, Sally Greene, Mr and Mrs Ian Hodgson, Mr and Mrs Norman Hudson, Phillip and Francesca Kendall, Mr E. Lloyd, Mrs Mogford, Mr David Moisey, John and Fiona Owen, David and Jennifer Powell, Mr and Mrs Ratcliffe, Mr and Mrs J. Reynolds, Mr and Mrs S. Riley-Smith, The Roald Dahl Foundation, Sancton Wood Junior School, Mr and Mrs Sands, John and Emma Simms-Hilditch, Andrew and Jessica Slater, Phillip and Barbara Stochtt, Sheila and Roger Storr, Mr and Mrs R. Swallow, Mrs Worsick and Wyevale Garden Centres.